Teachers' Notes for
BEAM's Big Book of

Word
Problems
for Years 5 and 6

Mike Askew

BEAM

BEAM Education

BEAM Education is a specialist mathematics education publisher, dedicated to promoting the teaching and learning of mathematics as interesting, challenging and enjoyable. Their materials cover teaching and learning needs from the age of 3 to 14 and they offer consultancy and training.
BEAM is an acknowledged expert in the field of mathematics education.

Published by BEAM Education
Maze Workshops
72a Southgate Road
London N1 3JT
info@beam.co.uk

Orders:
orderline 01242 267945
beamorders@nelsonthornes.com

www.beam.co.uk

© BEAM Education 2005
All rights reserved. None of the material in the Big Book may be reproduced or published in any form without prior permission from the publisher. The photocopiable worksheets in the Teachers' Notes may be reproduced by individual schools without permission from the publisher. No other material in the Teachers' Notes may be reproduced or published in any form without prior permission from the publisher. The CD-ROM may be used by individual schools as summarised in the Teachers' Notes.

Big Book and Teachers' Notes text © Mike Askew
The author's moral rights have been asserted.

ISBN 1 903142 81 4
British Library Cataloguing-in-Publication Data
Data available

Edited by Raewyn Glynn
Designed by Malena Wilson-Max

Big Book illustrations by Annabelle Hartmann, Mark Oliver and Anne Sharp
© Annabelle Hartmann
(Big Book pp 2, 7, 9, 11, 14, 19, 23, 24)
© Mark Oliver
(Big Book pp 1, 5, 8, 13, 16, 18, 20, 22)
© Anne Sharp
(Big Book pp 3, 4, 6, 10, 12, 15, 17, 21)

Printed in the UK by Cromwell Press Ltd

Contents

Introduction   5

Objectives   11

The 24 Units   13
   Year 5   14
   Year 6   38

Unit problem sheets   63
[photocopiables]
   Year 5   64
   Year 6   88

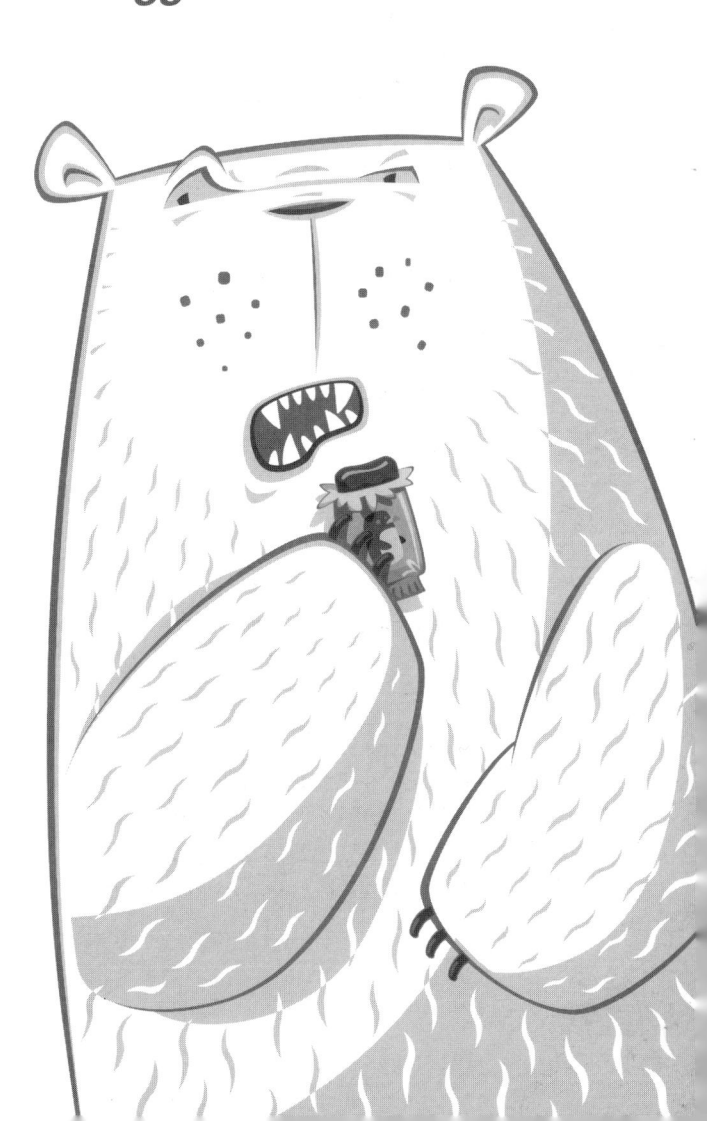

Introduction

This Word Problems resource comprises the Big Book, for use with children in Years 5 and 6, the Teachers' Notes (with photocopiable worksheets) and a CD-ROM.

The 24 Units in this resource provide a way of helping children move from being novice problem solvers to being expert problem solvers. Research has shown that there are some key differences between novice and expert problem solvers.

- **Novice problem solvers** look at the various parts of a problem and try to put them together to make sense of the problem.

- **Expert problem solvers** get an overall feel for what the problem is about and then seek out the parts that will help in a solution.

- **Novice problem solvers** treat each problem in isolation from other problems that they have worked on: they try to figure out what the problem is about simply by looking at the information given.

- **Expert problem solvers** treat each problem as being one of a generic class of problems: they ask themselves 'have I seen anything like this before?'

An example illustrates this. Consider the calculation 38 ÷ 6. Before reading on, try to think of a real world situation where the sensible answer to 38 ÷ 6 means rounding up the mathematical answer of 6 remainder 2 to 7.

Were you thinking of putting 38 eggs into egg boxes, or possibly people into mini-buses or tents? If not, your example is still probably not too far away from these. This is no mind-reading trick; many people choose problems of this sort for division situations where you need to round up.

These 24 units work on helping children to build up their knowledge of 'classes of problems' and the language to describe them. So when they meet a new problem they, like expert problem solvers, can think about what else they have seen that is similar and use appropriate language to describe the type of problem.

This approach is different from one that encourages strategies like looking for 'keywords'. The keywords approach rests on the assumption that the meaning of a problem somehow lies within the wording of the problem itself.
The expert/novice approach works on the assumption that the problem solver has to bring meaning to the wording of the problem. This is similar to research into reading and the idea that expert readers have mental 'frames' that they draw on in order to make sense of text. Consider, for example:

Sheila and Mike were excited as they finished decorating John's cake. They wondered if he would manage to blow out all the candles in one go.

The expert reader has no difficulty knowing that this is about preparing for a birthday party. But there is no mention of birthdays or parties: they bring that meaning to the words through the mental 'frame' they have for birthday parties.

Sheila and Mike started to put out sandwiches.
They each made 20 sandwiches and then put 4 sandwiches on each plate.
How many plates do they need altogether?

The expert problem solver recognises this as a one of the class of problems from their frame of 'division by grouping'. The novice, if they concentrate on the wording in the problem rather than the meaning they bring to it, is likely to add 20 and 4 as 'altogether means add'. (And knowing that 'each means divide' does not help, as 'each' is used with two different meanings.) These lessons help children develop such analogical reasoning. Expert problem solvers do use deductive thinking as well, and we need to encourage children in this way of thinking. But we also need to acknowledge the power of analogical thinking.

Teaching a Word Problem lesson

The 24 units are evenly split between Year 5 and Year 6. The first twelve units are designed for the younger age group, but you can use this structure flexibly. Some children in Year 5 will be able to go on to some of the Year 6 problems. Equally, some children in Year 6 may benefit from looking at the Year 5 problems.

You can integrate the 24 lessons with other lessons in one of two ways. Firstly, you could teach the Word Problem lessons following a regular pattern (once a fortnight, for example). The advantage of this is that the contents of each lesson have two weeks to 'simmer' in children's minds, so steady consolidation of the ideas takes place. Secondly, you could select specific Word Problem lessons and teach them alongside other lessons that deal with similar types of calculation. The objectives chart on page 11 is there to help you integrate the Word Problem lessons with other plans; the chart indicates the type of calculation covered by each problem.

Each Word Problem lesson in this resource takes the same basic form. This is so that children get used to what is expected of them in the lesson and they can then concentrate on thinking about the mathematics.

There are four parts to the lesson:

- solving the Big Book problems
- linking up the problems
- follow-up problems
- wrap-up.

Introduction

Solving the Big Book problems

Each page of the Big Book has three word problems on it. Working in pairs, or individually if they prefer, the children solve each of the problems in turn. Before moving on to the next problem there is a whole class discussion about the ways in which they interpreted the problem and the strategies used for solving it. The emphasis here is on direct teaching, not teaching directively. In other words, the role of the teacher is to support the children in their struggle to make sense of the problems rather than to explicitly direct them to use particular methods. When discussing the ways in which the children set about solving the problems, the role of the teacher is to support the children's explanations through asking clarifying questions, setting up models, pictures or diagrams, and to introduce notation that helps the other children understand a child's approach.

The pages in the Teachers' Notes provide specific suggestions for the sort of children's methods to look out for and ways to support the development of these.

Linking up the problems

In the second phase of the whole class introduction, the emphasis shifts from thinking about each problem separately to looking at the set of three and considering ways in which they are linked. On most of the Big Book pages, the three problems have been chosen to be representative of a class of problems. The second part of the whole class introduction is designed to draw children's attention to the common mathematical structure underlying the problems. This is supported by giving labels to classes of problems and using the imagery of the situations to help children build up their own archetypes for groups of problems.

Once again, the Teachers' Notes provide explicit guidance on what to focus the children's attention on.

Follow-up problems

After the initial whole class discussion of the Big Book problems and the links between them, the children then have time to work more independently on the ideas that have been introduced. There are two component parts to this next stage of the lesson.

One

Children work individually on follow-up problem sheets (given as photocopiables) that consolidate and develop the ideas introduced in the whole class part of the lesson. The problem sheets are provided here at two levels of difficulty (A and B). The level of difficulty is determined by the level of difficulty of the calculation involved. (The problem B sheets are numerically easier.) However, the basic mathematical structure of the word problem is the same on both sheets so that all children can focus on this aspect.

Two

Once they have done as much as they can independently, the children should join up with a partner and share their work. During this sharing, individuals are allowed to change their working and answers, but in ways that still preserve their own, original and independent working. Using a different coloured pen or pencil could help them make clear the distinction between their first workings and their workings with a partner. Erasers are definitely banned!

Wrap-up

Finally, the whole class comes back together again to further explore the nature of the problems and reinforce the key underlying ideas.

Classifying word problems

Expert problem solvers build up banks of images of 'archetypal' problems that serve as templates for sets of linked problems.

Classifying addition and subtraction problems

There are three main 'root' situations for addition and subtraction: change; combining and separating; and comparison. Although the distinctions between these three are somewhat blurred, they are useful for learning at this stage.

Change (increase/decrease)

Situations where there is an initial quantity and this is increased or decreased in some way are called 'change' problems.

I have 10p in my purse and put in another 5p. How much is in my purse now?
(Change 10 by adding on 5)

I have 10 jelly beans and eat 6. How many jelly beans do I have left?
(Change 10 by taking away 6)

Combining and separating

Situations where two sets are put together to create a new set that did not previously exist, or the reverse where a single set is split into two, are called 'combine/separate' problems.

Gran gave me 10p and grandad gave me 5p. How much do I have altogether?
(Combine 10 and 5)

I have 10 books in a pile and put 6 on the shelf. How many books are left in the pile?
(Separate the 10 into 6 and ...?)

Although to adults it appears obvious in each case (change and combine/separate) that the mathematical calculations are 10 + 5 and 10 − 6, to the novice learner this is not immediately obvious.

Comparison

Situations where nothing actually changes or is combined but where two sets are compared are called 'compare' problems.

I have 10p, Penny has 5p. How much more do I have?
(What is the difference between 10 and 5?)

I have 5p, Mark has 10p. How much more do I need to have the same as Mark?
(What is the difference between 10 and 5?)

Classifying multiplication and division problems

There are three main 'root' situations for multiplication: multiplication as repeated addition; multiplication as rate; and multiplication as scaling. Linked to this are two models of division: division as grouping (repeated subtraction); and division as sharing. Like addition and subtraction, the distinction between these is not firm, but the categorisation does provide a helpful model for teaching.

Multiplication as repeated addition

Situations where several groups all the same size need to be added together are called 'multiplication as repeated addition'.

A tray of cakes has 4 rows and 5 columns. How many cakes is that altogether?
(add 4 to itself 5 times or multiply 4 by 5 or add 5 to itself 4 times or multiply 5 by 4)

Every day for a week I put 12p into my money box. How much did I save that week?
(add 12 to itself 7 times or multiply 12 by 7)

Multiplication as rate

'Multiplication as rate' situations are ones where there is an implicit ratio, where, explicitly or implicitly, there is a 'per' in the context: wheels per tricycle, stickers per page, apples per bag.

I put 10 stickers on each (per) page of my album. I fill 8 pages.
How many stickers did I put in my album? (repeatedly add 10 or multiply 10 by 8)

A packet of biscuits contains 8 biscuits (8 per packet). I buy 4 packets.
Is that enough biscuits for 25 people to have one each?
(repeatedly add 8 or multiply 8 by 4)

Multiplication as scaling

'Multiplication as scaling' situations are ones where a continuous quantity is increased in size by a scaling factor.

When I got her, my pet grass snake was 5 centimetres long.
She is now 3 times as long as that. How long is she now? (5 multiplied by 3)

Introduction

*Last week my champion pumpkin weighed 3 kilograms.
Now it is 4 times as heavy. How heavy is it now? (3 multiplied by 4)*

Grouping (repeated subtraction)

Situations where an amount has to be put into equal sized groups or portions and the size of the group or portion is known in advance are known as 'division as grouping' or 'division as repeated subtraction'.

I have picked 45 apples. I put them into bags of 5. How many bags can I fill? (repeatedly subtract 5 from 45 or divide 45 by 5)

I have 21 m of rope and I want to make skipping ropes that are each 3 m long. How many can I make? (repeatedly subtract 3 from 21 or divide 21 by 3)

Division as sharing

Situations where an amount has to be put into equal sized groups and the number of group or portion is known in advance are known as 'division as sharing'.

*I have picked 35 apples. I have 5 bags to put them into.
How many apples can I put into each bag? (share 35 amongst 5 or divide 35 by 5)*

*I have 12 litres of juice and I want to put equal amounts into 6 jugs.
How much juice do I pour into each jug? (Share 12 amongst 6 or divide 12 by 6)*

Using the CD-ROM

The CD-ROM contains all the content in the Big Book. You can either project individual pages onto a whiteboard from your computer or print them out onto acetate sheets and use them on an overhead projector. The CD-ROM also contains all the problem sheets in the Teachers' Notes; this gives you the option of printing the sheets out, rather than making photocopies. In addition, there is an extra version of the problem sheets on the CD-ROM, with empty boxes in place of the numbers. This allows you to write in your own choice of numbers and to do further differentiation work – when you do this, select the numbers carefully, to retain the relationship between the problems on the same page.

In conclusion

Throughout your work on word problems, it is important to be explicit with children about the different kinds of calculation involved. Children can cope with these distinctions, once you have explained the features of a calculation, and compared one problem type with another. Sharing with children what in the past has effectively been 'secret knowledge' will help them understand the mathematics and develop appropriate problem-solving skills.

Objectives

Unit	Content objective	Problem-solving objective
Year 5		
1. Snowball	Recognise addition problems as both change and combine	Use and apply mental strategies for addition
2. Family shopping	Recognise addition problems as both change and combine	Use and apply mental strategies for addition
3. Snakes and Adders	Recognise compare problems (difference) as subtraction	Use and apply mental strategies for subtraction
4. Cyclops	Understand subtraction as 'taking away'	Identify change problems involving subtraction
5. Clown capers	Recognise multiplication as repeated addition problems	Use tables to record information
6. The magic cupboard	Recognise multiplication as rate problems	Use multiplication rather than repeated addition
7. Percy the builder	Recognise multiplication as array problems	Use tables to record information
8. Gardener's World	Recognise multiplication as scaling problems	Use and apply knowledge of multiplication bonds
9. Village fête	Recognise division as repeated subtraction (grouping)	Use the relationship between multiplication and division
10. Gods and goddesses	Recognise division as sharing problems	Use and apply the relationship between multiplication and division
11. Reunion	Understanding division as repeated subtraction	Deciding whether to round up or round down an answer, depending on the context
12. Thor, the god of thunder	Recognise which operation to use when solving word problems	Consolidate different problem classifications
Year 6		
13. Sea escapades	Recognise addition problems as both change and combine	Use and apply mental strategies for addition
14. Les bicyclettes	Recognise addition problems as both change and combine	Use and apply mental strategies for addition
15. Gnoming around	Recognise compare problems (difference) as subtraction	Use and apply mental strategies for subtraction
16. Airport	Understand subtraction as 'taking away'	Identify change problems involving subtraction
17. Changing Pelts	Recognise multiplication as repeated addition problems	Use tables to record information
18. Witsend Towers	Recognise multiplication as rate problems	Use multiplication rather than repeated addition
19. Planting out	Recognise multiplication as array problems	Use tables to record information
20. Planet Zog	Recognise multiplication as scaling problems	Use and apply knowledge of multiplication bonds
21. Verger Records	Recognise division as repeated subtraction (grouping)	Recognise the relationship between multiplication and division
22. Party time	Recognise division as sharing problems	Use and apply the relationship between multiplication and division
23. Dan the Dragon Slayer	Understanding division as repeated subtraction	Deciding whether to round up or round down an answer, depending on the context
24. Lords of the Bling	To recognise which operation to use when solving word problems	To consolidate different problem classifications

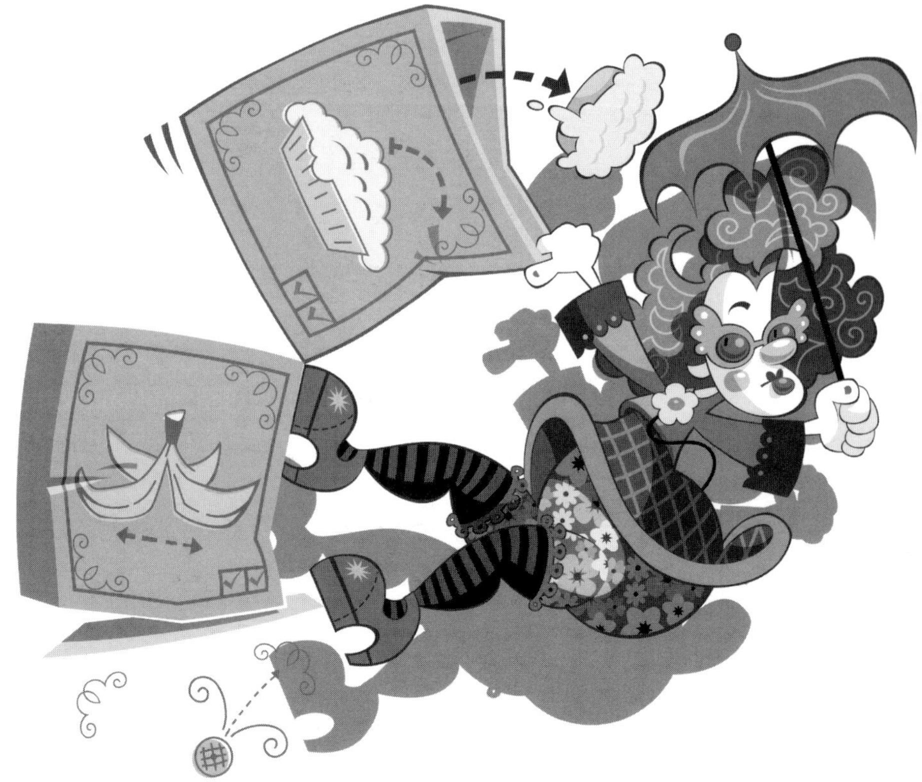

The 24 Units

Year 5

Unit 1	**Snowball**	14
Unit 2	**Family shopping**	16
Unit 3	**Snakes and Adders**	18
Unit 4	**Cyclops**	20
Unit 5	**Clown capers**	22
Unit 6	**The magic cupboard**	24
Unit 7	**Percy the builder**	26
Unit 8	**Gardener's World**	28
Unit 9	**Village fête**	30
Unit 10	**Gods and goddesses**	32
Unit 11	**Reunion**	34
Unit 12	**Thor, the god of thunder**	36

Year 6

Unit 13	**Sea escapades**	38
Unit 14	**Les bicyclettes**	40
Unit 15	**Gnoming around**	42
Unit 16	**Airport**	44
Unit 17	**Changing Pelts**	46
Unit 18	**Witsend Towers**	48
Unit 19	**Planting out**	50
Unit 20	**Planet Zog**	52
Unit 21	**Verger Records**	54
Unit 22	**Party time**	56
Unit 23	**Dan the Dragon Slayer**	58
Unit 24	**Lords of the Bling**	60

Snowball

Objectives
- Recognise addition problems as both change and combine
- Use and apply mental strategies for addition

Big Book problems

The three problems here are all addition problems. Two of them (1 and 3) are 'combine' problems: two separate quantities are joined together to make a third total amount. Problem 2 is subtly different as it is a 'change' problem: given an initial amount, this is increased in some way. Identifying addition problems is usually quite straightforward as the structure of such problems usually mirrors the mathematical sentence to be written down. The aim of the lesson is to help children recognise addition problems and talk about them as either 'combine' or 'change' problems.

Whole class

Problem 1

As the children are working, make a note of any pairs who reverse the order of the numbers and start with 435. If no pair has used this method, then point it out yourself.

Ask if anyone can come and write a mathematical sentence for this problem and help the children record:

  131 + 435 = ☐

or

  435 + 131 = ☐

Some children may benefit from being shown how the empty number line can support their mental calculation here.

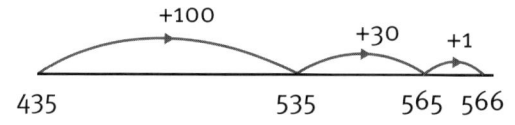

```
           +100        +30   +1
       ⌒──────────⌒────⌒──⌒
      435         535  565 566
```

Problem 2

This time, look out for pairs of children who appear to find the answer by adding the 52 and 8 first and then adding 60 to 246.

Discuss this method and why it might be easier than trying to add the 52 and 246 first. As before, establish that an appropriate sentence is:

  52 + 246 + 8 = ☐

which is equivalent to:

  52 + 8 + 246

Unit 1

This latter arrangement of the numbers, together with the fact that 240 + 60 = 300, means that an using an empty number line should not be necessary. However, if any children are having difficulty, model this on the empty number line.

Problem 3

The numbers here are more awkward than those in the previous problems, so encourage the children to use an empty number line to support their reasoning. Bridging through 200 simplifies adding 40 to 192.

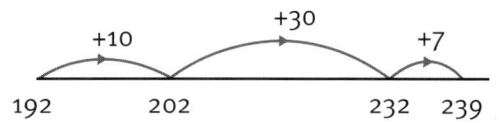

```
        +10        +30        +7
      ──────>  ──────────>  ────>
    192       202         232  239
```

Linking up the problems

Ask the children to look at all three problems and discuss with their partner what they all have in common.

Apart from being about the Snowball, the children should be able to notice that they are all addition problems. Point out to them that two of the problems were combine problems that involved two amounts that needed to be put together or combined to give the final total. And one of the problems was a change problem where an initial quantity was changed in some way. Can they sort out which was which?

Follow-up problems

Pairs

Give out problem sheets A and B.

As the children are working, encourage them to write down appropriate mathematical sentences.

Question 4 on each sheet is a subtraction problem. The children should not find it difficult to see that this question is different and explain why in Question 6.

Ask any children who finish quickly to write their own addition problem to swap with a partner.

Wrap up

Whole class

For each sheet, ask the children which one of the questions was not an addition problem and how they knew.

Family shopping

Objectives
- Recognise addition problems as both change and combine
- Use and apply mental strategies for addition

Big Book problems

Like the 'Snowball' problems, these three problems have the same structure and are all addition problems. However, the structure of the problems is a little more complicated than in the previous unit.

Problem 1 follows the usual structure of an addition problem where the result of combining two quantities has to be found. Problem 3 is an addition as change problem, but rather than finding the result of the change the children have to establish what the change is. Thus, although an addition problem, this could be solved by subtraction. Problem 2 has the most difficult structure. This is another addition as change problem, but the change and end result are given, so the children have to find the starting amount.

Whole class

Problem 1

As the children are working, make a note of any pairs who calculate:

   12.50 + 24.50 = ☐

and then adjust the result by subtracting 5p from their answer. Make sure that one such pair is amongst those invited to come to the front to explain their method.

If no pair has used this method, model it yourself. Use the empty number line to help show the structure of the solution method, starting off by pointing out that 12.50 + 24.50 is equivalent to 24.50 + 12.50.

Point out to the children that this method involves finding an answer to a simpler calculation and then adjusting the result.

Problem 2

Encourage the children to use an empty number line to support their reasoning here. Two methods of solution are likely:

   starting with 7.45 and adding on to this to reach 21
   or
   starting at 21 and subtracting 7.45

If a pair has used either method encourage them to explain their reasoning. Otherwise model both yourself using an empty number line.

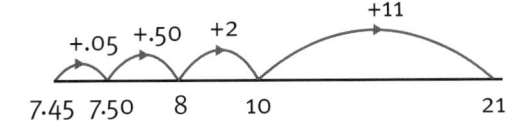

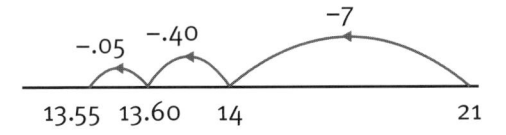

Discuss with the children that there are three equivalent mathematical sentence linked to the problem:

☐ + £7.45 = £21

£7.45 + ☐ = £21

£12 − £7.45 = ☐

Problem 3

The structure of this problem makes it likely that the children will count on from 15.36 to 25. The empty number line is particularly helpful here.

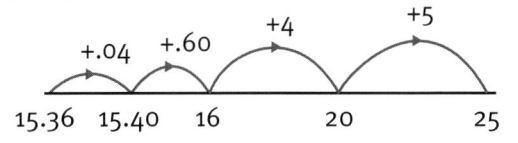

```
       +.04  +.60   +4      +5
      ⌒     ⌒     ⌒       ⌒
   15.36 15.40  16      20       25
```

Discuss number sentence that arises from this problem:

£15.36 + ☐ = £25

What are other number sentences that are equivalent to this?

Linking up the problems

Turn back to the page of 'Snowball' problems.

Can anyone remember what all those problems had in common?

Return to these problems. Ask the children to look at all three problems and discuss with their partner why they could also all be described as addition problems, even if they used subtraction to solve some of them.

Follow-up problems

Pairs

Give out problem sheets A and B.

As the children are working, encourage them to write down appropriate mathematical sentences.

Question 5 on each sheet is a multiplication problem.

Ask any children who finish quickly to write their own addition problem to swap with a partner.

Wrap up

Whole class

For each sheet, ask the children to explain why they thought Question 5 was different to the rest.

Snakes and Adders

Objectives

- Recognise compare problems (difference) as subtraction
- Use and apply mental strategies for subtraction

Big Book problems

Whole class

All three problems here can be solved by subtraction. The first problem is different from the other two as it involves a change situation (the length of the rattlesnake after it had its tail chopped off) and is more likely quickly to be recognised by the children as subtraction. The other two problems are subtraction situations that involve comparing two amounts and finding the difference. In Problem 3 this is reasonably clear. Problem 2 is more complicated as the difference is given rather than having to be found. Each of these last two problems can be modeled either by adding on or subtracting.

Problem 1

For this first problem, ask the children NOT to work out the answer, but simply to write down the mathematical sentence that they are going to find the answer to in order to solve the problem. The children should not have too much difficulty in establishing:

$390 - 155 = \square$

as an appropriate sentence.

Now ask them to work out the answer. Invite children to share their methods. If anyone suggests that they found the answer by counting up from 155 to 390, show how they might have recorded this as:

$155 + \square = 390.$

Other methods to encourage include subtracting 150 from 390 and then subtracting 5.

Model both of these on the empty number line if appropriate.

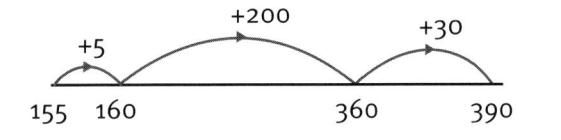

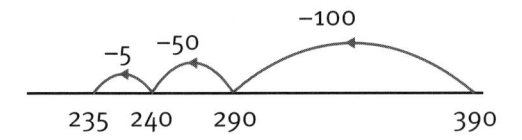

Problem 2

Ask the children to work in pairs to find a solution and to be prepared to explain their method. Watch out for children who misinterpret the problem and think that they have to subtract 78 from 92. A quick sketch showing the relationship between Robbie and Sue may help them understand the relationship between their lengths.

Once the children have sorted out the relationship of the lengths it is likely that they will set up the mathematical sentence:

$92 + 78 = \square$

Unit 3

that the situation can also be thought of in terms of subtraction and set up the sentence:

$\square - 78 = 92$

$45 + \square = 79$

Problem 3

Ask the children to work in pairs to find a solution and to be prepared to explain their method.

Strategies that the children are likely to use include:

- subtracting 720 from 900 and adding 8 back on to the answer
- counting up from 720 to 908.

Establish that there are two different mathematical sentences that they could use to record the calculations:

$908 - 720 = \square$

$720 + \square = 908$

Linking up the problems

Point out to the children that each of the problems could be represented by a subtraction sentence

$390 - 155 = \square, \quad 908 - 720 = \square, \quad \square - 78 = 92$

Tell them that Problem 1 was different to the other two problems and ask them to talk with their partner about why this was so.

Discuss the nature of the difference, pointing out that Problem 1 was a change problem that involved something being removed, but that the other two involved some sort of comparing: nothing was taken away or changed, but two sets were compared.

Follow-up problems

Pairs

Give out problem sheets A and B.

As the children are working on the problem sheets, encourage them to write down appropriate mathematical sentences. Encourage children who are having difficulty to set up a diagram of the situation or to model it on the empty number line.

Wrap up

Whole class

Invite children to share with the class the problems that they wrote. Does the class agree that these are compare problems?

Work with the class on writing up a description of the difference between a subtraction as take away problem and a subtraction as compare problem.

19

Cyclops

Objectives
- Understand subtraction as 'taking away'
- Identify change problems involving subtraction

Big Book problems

These problems have the same structure as change problems involving a decrease and with the result unknown. Each problem contains a quantity that has to be reduced to find a total amount. The structure of the first two problems is quite straightforward and children should have few difficulties solving them and writing an appropriate mathematical sentence. The third problem is more difficult as it is the amount that was subtracted that has to be calculated, rather than the end amount.

Whole class

Problem 1

It should be easy for the children in their pairs to relate the 'action' of this problem (that is, part of a quantity being destroyed) to subtraction and to write down the mathematical sentence:

127 − 35 = ☐

As children share their methods, you might want to remind them that an empty number line can help them keep track of their working if they are not confident of holding all the information in their heads. Also support the less confident children to bridge through the 100 in subtracting 35.

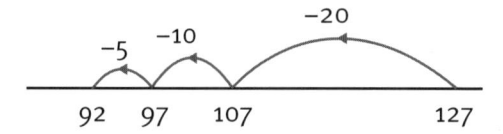

Problem 2

Here again, this should not present too many difficulties. Ask one of the children to come and write the mathematical sentence on the board and then show how this could be modelled on the empty number line.

373 − 80 = ☐

Problem 3

Once pairs have found a solution to this problem, help children use the relationship between addition and subtraction to set up different mathematical sentences:

220 − ☐ = 55

or

55 + ☐ = 220

Unit 4

As before, model this on the empty number line by counting back from 220 to 55.

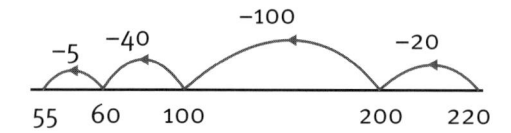

```
       -5    -40        -100              -20
       ↶      ↶      ↶                    ↶
    ────┴──────┴──────────────────────────┴────
       55  60  100                  200  220
```

You can also show how, starting from the sentence 55 − ☐ = 220, this can be modeled on the empty number line as finding the difference between the two numbers by counting on.

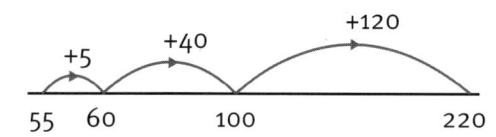

```
                         +120
              +5   +40
              ↷    ↷          ↷
    ──────────┴────┴──────────────────────────
              55  60  100                 220
```

Discuss with the children which they think is the easier method: counting back from 220 or counting on from 55. Point out that although the word problem actually involved taking away, to solve the mathematical sentence they might choose to do something different (count on).

Linking up the problems

Ask the children to look at all three problems and discuss with their partner what they all have in common.

Apart from being about Cyclops, the children should be able to notice that they are all subtraction problems. Point out to them that they are all subtraction as take away problems: that each problem involved an amount that needed to be changed in some way to find the answer.

Follow-up problems

Pairs

Give out problem sheets A and B.

As the children are working, encourage them to write down appropriate mathematical sentences. Encourage children who are having difficulties keeping track of their working to use an empty number line to record their thinking.

Question 3 on each sheet is not really a problem at all. It is there to make the point that they need to read questions carefully and not assume they know what is expected either because of the pattern of the worksheet or because of the numbers involved.

Ask any children who finish quickly to try and write down what is meant by a change problem.

Wrap up

Whole class

Ask children to share with the class the change problems that they wrote. Is everyone convinced that each one is a change problem? How do they know?

Clown capers

Objectives
- Recognise multiplication as repeated addition problems
- Use tables to record information

Big Book problems

Whole class

These three problems are the first that deal with multiplication. All three problems here are relatively straightforward. The emphasis in the teaching and discussing should be on the links to recording these as multiplication sentences and effective ways of working out the calculations.

Problem 1

Ask the children to work either on their own or with a partner to try and figure out the solution to the problem. As they work, make a note of different methods that they use so that you can call upon particular individuals to come and share their method with the class. In particular, watch out for children who need to add together 4 lots of 24 and anyone who carried out the multiplication by 4 by doubling and doubling again. Work with the children on recording the calculation as:

$24 \times 4 = 96$

Point out that since there were 24 custard pies in one box and there were four boxes, that is why you need to add 24 to itself 4 times or multiply 24 by 4.

Did anyone spot that 25 x 4 = 100 and use this to find the answer?

Problem 2

Treat this problem in the same way as problem one, establishing the appropriate number sentence of:

$48 \times 50 = 240$

Children are likely to have found the answer to this in two different ways:

- by multiplying 48 by 10 and then multiplying the answer by 5
- by multiplying 48 by 100 and then halving the answer

Discuss both of these methods with the children and ask which they think was easier.

Problem 3

Follow the same approach here as in the previous two problems, setting up the number sentence of:

$8 \times 15 = 120$

Discuss two possible ways of finding the solution to this:

- 8 multiplied by 15 can be found by calculating 8 multiplied by 10 and 8 multiplied by 5 and adding the two answers together.

Unit 5

- Using the knowledge that multiplication is commutative to answer the equivalent calculation of 15 × 8. This can be calculated by doubling 15 (30), doubling 30 (60) and then doubling once more (120).

Linking up the problems

Go back to Problem 1 and record the working in the form of a simple table.

Boxes	Pies
1	24
4	96

Record again the associated multiplication 24 × 4. Talk through how, reading down the table, the 1 became 4 times bigger and so the 24 also had to be multiplied by 4.

Ask the children to have a go at drawing up the table for the second problem. When they have had a minute or two to do this, work through setting up, using the table to record the intermediate step of multiplying by 100:

Boxes	Squirting flowers
1	48
100	480
50	240

Again, talk through the multiplicative relationships between the numbers in the columns: the one becomes 100 times bigger (is multiplied by 100) so the 48 needs to be made 100 times bigger, then the 100 is halved to 50 so the 480 must be halved.

Repeat this for Problem 3.

Boxes	Banana skins
1	48
2	480
4	240
8	120

Follow-up problems

Pairs

The follow-up problems all follow a very similar format to the Big Book problems and the children should not have too many difficulties in finding answers, even if their methods are not the most efficient. The children are not expected to put the information into table form, but if you think any of them could cope with this, then encourage them to do so.

Wrap up

Class

Go over one or two of the problems that the children made up for themselves. Work on recording these as multiplications and also putting the information in the form of a table.

The magic cupboard

Objectives
- Recognise multiplication as rate problems
- Use multiplication rather than repeated addition

Big Book problems

Whole class

Although, on the surface, these problems look very similar to multiplication as repeated addition they are subtly different. While these problems can be solved using repeated addition, the underlying contexts that give rise to the calculations are themselves not repeated addition situations. Here the contexts are all ones where some sort of rate is involved: numbers of bugs per apple, orange or pear. In the previous two units the total number of items were always present from the beginning. Hence the items could, in theory, be taken out and counted. In rate problems the final number of items does not pre-exist the calculation, but is created within the context.

These differences are not explicitly explored with the children, but both this and the next unit build on the use of tables introduced in the previous two units to help the children develop an intuitive feel for such situations.

Problem 1

Put this partially completed table on the board and ask if anyone can explain the relationship between the table and the information given in the problem:

Number of apples	Number of maggots
1	6

Discuss how the table shows the number of worms that each apple was turned into. Ask the children how many apples Marge transformed and how they could build up the table to find the answer.

Number of apples	Number of maggots
1	6
8	48
16	

Ask the children to discuss with their partner what they think the final missing number in the table should be and why they have come up with that answer. Discuss what the missing number is and establish that it is 96. Leave the table up on the board for the rest of the lesson.

Problem 2

Put this table on the board and ask the children if they can complete the first row:

Number of oranges	Number of maggots

Unit 6

Establish that the top row entries should be 1 and 5 as Marge turns every one orange into 5 maggots. Ask the children what might be a good intermediate calculation to make in going from 1 orange to 14 oranges. Once you have agreed that 7 would be a suitable intermediate step, ask the children to work in pairs to figure out the final number. Again, leave the completed table on the board as a prompt for later in the lesson.

Number of oranges	Number of maggots
1	5
7	
14	

Problem 3

Deal with this problem in the same way as Problem 2, putting up the empty table and working with the children on filling in the first row, the first column, multiplying by 9 as an intermediate step and then adding the final missing figure.

Linking up the problems

Direct the children's attention back to Problem 1. Work with the children on recording the calculation that they carried out as:

6 x 16 = 80 (6 worms for each one of 16 apples, hence 6 multiplied by 16)

(Note: while we can read the table differently – 16 apples each replaced by 6 worms, or 16 x 6, the above interpretation is consistent with what the children have been doing in the previous unit.)

Ask pairs to record their calculation for Problem 2 as a multiplication sentence:

5 x 14 = 70 (5 maggots for every orange, 14 oranges transformed, hence 5 multiplied by 14)

Repeat this for Problem 3, setting up the calculation 7 x 18 = 126. Point out that all three problems are multiplication situations.

Follow-up problems

Pairs

Ask the children to draw up tables for the problems that need them. Warn them that one of the problems does not need a table to be drawn up, so they will only be drawing up five tables. Problem 5 is the rogue problem being a subtraction (change) problem. Some children may feel that they do not need to draw up the tables to find the answer. Acknowledge with them that that is fine, but that they will need to be able to use the tables later so you would like them to draw them up even if they do not feel the need.

Wrap up

Whole class

Ask the children for examples of the problems that they made up using the table in Question 6.

Percy the builder

Objectives
- Recognise multiplication as array problems
- Use tables to record information

Big Book problems

Whole class

The structure of these three problems is very similar to that of the problems in 'Clown capers', but whereas those situations were based on repeated addition, the ones here arise from multiplication as arrays. Once again, simple tables are used to record the information.

Problem 1

Remind the children of the work that you did on the last unit and in particular how the information in the questions could be recorded in the form of a table. Work with the class on setting up an appropriate table for the first problem, with intermediate steps.

Number of rows	Number of bricks
1	13
10	
5	
15	

Ask the children to work either on their own or with a partner to try and figure out the solution to the problem.

Point out that as there were 13 bricks in one row and there were 15 rows, you need to multiply 13 by 15. Link this to the table: reading down the table, the 1 became 15 times bigger and so the 13 also has been multiplied by 13.

Problem 2

Treat this problem in the same way as Problem 1, starting off by asking the children to work in pairs and draw up an appropriate table to record the information and intermediate steps.

Number of rows	Number of wall tiles
1	26
10	
2	
4	
14	

26 × 14 (26 multiplied by 14)

Unit 7

Problem 3

Follow the same approach here as in the previous two problems, setting up the models of:

Number of rows	Number of floor tiles
1	34
10	
2	
12	

As before, establish that the appropriate multiplication sentence is 34 × 12 and link this to reading down the columns of the table: we go from 1 row to 12 rows, so we have multiplied by 12 the 34 tiles that there are in one row.

Linking up the problems

Go back over the tables drawn up for each problem, recapping on how to interpret these by reading down the columns. Put up the following table:

Number of rows	Number of bricks
1	5
18	

Ask the children to talk to their partner for a minute or two and to decide what the wording of the problem might have been that gave rise to this table. Invite children to share their problems with the class.

Follow-up problems

Pairs

The follow-up problems all follow a very similar format to the Big Book problems and the children should not have too many difficulties in finding answers, even if their methods are not the most efficient.

This time, the children are expected to put the information into table form. Do not worry if they do this before or after solving the problems, it is simply to get them used to recording the information in this form.

Question 4 is an addition (combine) problem, there to check that the children are thinking about the wording of the problems and not simply falling into a formulaic approach.

Wrap up

Whole class

Go over one or two of the problems that the children made up for themselves.
Work on recording these as multiplications and checking that they reflect the information in the table.

Gardener's World

Objectives
- Recognise multiplication as scaling problems
- Use and apply knowledge of multiplication bonds

Big Book problems

Whole class

So far, the children have been introduced to three different models of multiplication: multiplication as repeated addition, multiplication as rate, and multiplication as an array. These three models were linked by putting the information into table form.

This unit deals with the model of multiplication as scaling. Through the context of comparing quantities, children are encouraged to think of such comparisons as a scaling up: in other words, to think of them multiplicatively rather than additively.

Problem 1

Read through this problem with the children and ask them to discuss with a partner what they think the solution is. This problem should not cause the children too many difficulties. Invite pairs to explain how they worked out the answer. Did anyone use a table to help them keep track of their workings? In particular, emphasise thinking about the solution as multiplication: the marrow is six times as heavy as it was so the original weight of 34 g needs to be multiplied by 6:

$34 \times 6 = 204$

Problem 2

As with Problem 1, after reading it through with the children get them to discuss the solution in pairs. The important thing to emphasise is the link between the way in which the onion is seven times as heavy as Eddie and the associated mathematical sentence of:

$18 \times 18 = 324$

Problem 3

Treat this problem in the same fashion as Problems 1 and 2. Once again, downplay any discussion of additive methods of solution. Pay most attention to the fact that the leek is five times longer than it originally was, so the appropriate mathematical sentence is:

$28 \times 5 = 140$

Unit 8

Linking up the problems

Ask the children to work in pairs and discuss what is similar about all three problems. Draw out the key idea that each problem involves making a comparison between two quantities.

Point out to the children that the problems did not say how much heavier or longer one vegetable was than it had been, but instead indicated how many times heavier or longer they had become. Introduce the language of scaling: that the weight of the marrow needed to be scaled up by a multiple of 6. Can the children use the language of scaling to talk about the other problems in a similar way?

Follow-up problems

Pairs

All but one of the problems follows a similar format in dealing with scalings. However, Question 5 is different in that it is a compare (difference) problem rather than a scaling problem. This may cause some children a bit of difficulty – the length has changed and they may want to multiply as they did in Question 4.

Drawing a diagram for each of the questions may help the children appreciate the difference between a compare situation where the comparison is expressed in terms of a scaling (so many times longer) and a compare situation where the comparison is expressed in terms of addition (so much longer).

Wrap up

Whole class

Discuss with the children their explanations and reasons for why Jo was wrong in his thinking on Question 5. Explore the idea that, although there is a comparison of lengths, this comparison is expressed in terms of how much longer rather than how many times longer.

Village fête

Objectives

- Recognise division as repeated subtraction (grouping)
- Use the relationship between multiplication and division

This is the first of the units dealing with division. It works on the model of division as repeated subtraction: given 300 ml of juice to pour into cups of 25 ml, how many cups can be filled? This is complemented in the next unit by the model of division as 'sharing': given 300 items, if these are shared between 25 bags, how many items are in each bag?

Big Book problems

Whole class

Problem 1

In pairs, ask the children to work together and figure out the answer. Invite children to offer their solutions and methods of arriving at them. Remind them of the types of tables they have been drawing up and ask them to draw up a table to represent the information in the problem. Work with the class on establishing that an appropriate table is:

Number of glasses	Amount of juice
1	25 ml
	300 ml

and that there are two ways of thinking about the missing number:

down the columns: what do you have to multiply the 25 by to get to 300

or

across the rows: the 1 has been multiplied by 25 so the 300 must be divided by 5

In this case, thinking down the columns is easier and the children may want to fill in some additional steps. Leave the table on the board for the children to refer to.

Number of glasses	Amount of juice
1	25 ml
10	250 ml
2	50 ml
12	300 ml

Problem 2

Again, set the pairs off to work out the solution. As before, get some children to share their methods. Work with the class on drawing up a relationship table to model the second problem and compare it with the first.

Number of bags	Amount of sherbert
1	15 g
	195 g

Unit 9

It is likely that many children will have solved this problem by implicitly saying 'what do I need to multiply 15 by to get 180?'

$15 \times \square = 180$

This relates to the figures in the table by reading 'down' the table. Again, the solution can be found by adding in intermediate steps.

Number of bags	Amount of sherbert
1	15 g
10	150 g
3	45 g
13	195 g

Problem 3

Reveal Problem 3 and ask the children to draw up a table and appropriate calculations. Go over their solutions, discussing how they could use the information to find the solution.

Discuss how the table and calculations are still similar to those for Problems 1 and 2 even though the 'real world' situation is different. The added complication here is that the total length of 290 cm cannot be cut up into 20 cm lengths exactly. Building up the table will allow the children to see how close to 290 they can get.

Number of pieces	Length of licorice
1	120 cm
10	200 cm
4	80 cm
14	280 cm

Linking up the problems

After the problems have been solved, ask the children to discuss with their partner what is common to the three problems. Discuss with the class that both are division problems and involve subtracting equal amounts.

Follow-up problems

Pairs

Give out problem sheets A and B. The children set up and fill in the relationship tables for the first four problems and make up their own problems for the table given in the last two problems. Encourage them to write down appropriate mathematical sentences and reinforce the idea that they can use either multiplication or division to reach a solution.

Wrap up

Whole class

Invite two or three pairs to share their problems with the class. Can the class decide when they think it is more appropriate to use division rather than multiplication?

Gods and goddesses

Objectives
- Recognise division as sharing problems
- Use and apply the relationship between multiplication and division

This is the second of the units dealing with division. In contrast to the previous unit, this works on the model of division as sharing. This is likely to be a more familiar model for the children and Problems 1 and 2 should not present them with too many difficulties. Problem 3 is like the ones in the previous units and is a division as repeated subtraction (grouping). Careful use of relationship tables should help the children to sort out the information in the problems.

Big Book problems

Class

Problem 1

In pairs, ask the children to work together and figure out the answer.

Invite children to offer their solutions and methods of arriving at them. Once again, remind them of the sorts of tables they have been drawing up and ask them to draw up a table to represent the information in the problem.

Work with the class on establishing that an appropriate table is:

Number of hands	Number of apples
1	
8	128

It is likely that many children will have solved this problem by saying 'what do I need to multiply 8 by to get 128?' and working with trial and improvement:

$8 \times \square = 128$

This relates to the figures in the table by reading 'across' the table, noting that whatever the 8 had to be multiplied by to get 128, the 1 in the first column has to be multiplied by the same number to preserve the relationship.

Point out that the table can also be read from bottom to top: the relationship of the 8 to the 1 is that the 1 is 8 times smaller, or the 8 is divided by 8. So the 128 must also be divided by 8:

$128 \div 8 \times \square$

This number sentence can be solved by subtracting multiples of 8 from 128.

Leave the table on the board for the children to refer to.

Problem 2

Again, set the pairs off to work out the solution. As before, get some children to share their methods. Work with the class on drawing up a relationship table to model the second problem and comparing it with the first.

Unit 10

Number of hands	Number of feathers
1	
16	128

As in Problem 1, explore the relationships between reading down the columns of the table and across the rows.

Did anyone spot that since Pomelo has twice as many arms as Arancia and the number of feathers is the same as the number of apples, then the answer to this problem must be half the previous one?

Problem 3

Ask the children to draw up a relationship table and appropriate calculations for this problem.

The structure of this problem is different to the previous two. As children complete their tables, encourage them to talk about them in different ways: across the rows from left to right and right to left, up and down the columns.

Number of hands	Number of fish
1	15
	180

One way to tackle the solution here is to put in additional rows and multiply up to 180.

Number of hands	Number of fish
1	15
10	150
3	30
0	180

Follow-up problems

Pairs

Give out problem sheets A and B. Three of the problems are division as sharing problems while the other two are division as equal grouping or repeated subtraction problems. In both cases, drawing up relationship tables should help the children keep track of the information.

As the children are working, encourage them to write down appropriate mathematical sentences and reinforce the idea that they can use either multiplication or division to reach a solution depending on how they 'read' the information in their tables.

Wrap up

Whole class

Discuss the two different models of multiplication: repeated subtraction (equal grouping) and sharing. Can the children explain how they would be able to tell the difference between the two?

Reunion

Objectives
- Understanding division as repeated subtraction
- Deciding whether to round up or round down an answer, depending on the context

Big Book problems

Whole class

These problems introduce the children to the need to look at the mathematical solution to a problem and decide whether or not that is a sensible solution to the contextual situation from which the calculation arose. This is done using division problems where there is a need to either round up or round down the numerical answer to arrive at a sensible solution.

Problem 1

Set the pairs off to work out the solution. As they are working, note the different methods they use and select the two or three pairs that you will invite to demonstrate their method.

When two or three methods have been shown, ask the children what number sentence(s) they could write to express the calculation they carried out. Put these on the board. Some may suggest:

$4 \times 12 = 48$

and if it is not forthcoming from the children, put up:

$50 \div 4 = 12 \text{ r } 2$.

Discuss with the children the difference between the mathematical solution (12 r 2) and the problem solution and whether the sensible answer to the problem is 12 r 2, 12 or 13.

Problem 2

Repeat the above for Problem 2. Once again, get:

$50 \div 6 = 8 \text{ r } 2$

on the board and discuss what the sensible answer to the problem is (8).

Problem 3

As before, set the pairs off to work out the solution. As they are working, note the different methods they use and select the two or three pairs that you will invite to demonstrate their method.

Once again, some may suggest:

$12 \times 4 = 48$

and if it is not forthcoming from the children, put up:

$13 \times 15 = 52$.

Discuss with the children whether the sensible answer to the problem is 13 r 5, 13 or 14.

Unit 11

Linking up the problems

Ask the children in their pairs to discuss and jot down:

- ways in which the problems are alike
- ways in which the problems are different

Discuss their various suggestions for similarities and differences. In particular, draw out:

- all the problems involved division
- the answers to 1 and 3 were rounded up, while the answer to 2 was rounded down

Follow-up problems

Pairs

Give out problem sheets A and B.

The children work out the solutions, and decide whether they had to round up or round down to give a sensible answer to the problem.

As the children are working, encourage them to write down appropriate mathematical sentences and reinforce the idea that repeated subtraction leads to division.

Question 3 on each sheet is a subtraction problem, so that the children do not assume that all the questions are division ones.

Wrap up

Whole class

Invite two or three pairs to share their problems with the class. Can the class decide which is the round up problem and which is the round down problem?

Display other pairs of problems on the problem board, with the invitation to decide which are round up problems and which are round down problems.

Thor, the god of thunder

Objectives
- Recognise which operation to use when solving word problems
- Consolidate different problem classifications

This unit presents a 'mixed bag' of problems. As the children work on them, they need to be encouraged to see if they can remember if the problems are like any that they have encountered before.

Big book problems

Class

As the children work through each problem in turn, concentrate on discussing the calculation strategies that they used. Then, when they have finished all three problems, discuss what type of problem each was.

Problem 1

This is a multiplication as scaling problem and the children should not have too much difficulty in setting up the calculation:

50 × 12

Watch out for two different calculation strategies here: multiplying 12 by 100 and then halving the answer and multiplying 50 × 10, 50 × 2 and adding the two answers. Which do the children prefer?

Problem 2

This problem is a change problem, but the wording of the problem is quite complex: it is not 128 − 108 but 128 + 108 that needs to be calculated. Getting children to act out the situation may help anyone who is having difficulty understanding what is going on.

Problem 3

This is a division as repeated subtraction problem. It will help reinforce the link between this and multiplication problems if you set up a table to show the information.

Number of clouds	Number of thunderbolts
1	9
0	108

Unit 12

Linking up the problems

Ask the children to work in pairs and discuss what type of problem each one was.

Can they remember any of the names for different types of problems introduced over the previous lessons?

Problems 1 and 3 are both multiplication and division problems: Problem 1 involves a scaling, Problem 3 involves division as repeated subtraction or grouping. Problem 2 is a change problem. Put these terms up on the board for the children to refer to when solving the follow-up problems.

Follow-up problems

Pairs

As well as finding solutions to the problems, the children should try and identify what type of problem each example represents. The best way to structure this would be to get them to work on their own to solve the problems and then to work in pairs and discuss each one in turn to decide what type of problem it is.

Questions 1, 3 and 4 are all multiplication as scaling problems; Question 2 is change (subtraction); Question 5 is also a subtraction, but is finding the difference; Question 6 is a simple multiplication, but with several distracting pieces of information.

Wrap up

Whole class

Go over the follow-up problems, discussing what type each one is.

Sea escapades

Objectives
- Recognise addition problems as both change and combine
- Use and apply mental strategies for addition

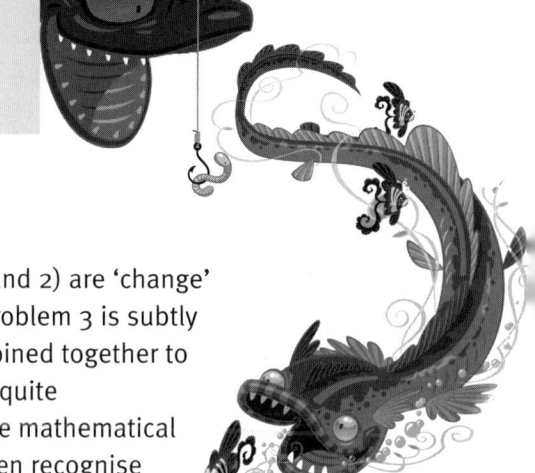

Big Book problems

The three problems here are all addition problems. Two of them (1 and 2) are 'change' problems: given an initial amount, this is increased in some way. Problem 3 is subtly different as it is a 'combine' problem: two separate quantities are joined together to make a third total amount. Identifying addition problems is usually quite straightforward as the structure of such problems usually mirrors the mathematical sentence to be written down. The aim of the lesson is to help children recognise addition problems and talk about them as either 'combine' or 'change' problems.

Class

Problem 1

As the children are working, make a note of any pairs who spot that 400 + 600 = 1000 and so start by adding these two numbers. If no pair has used this method, then point it out yourself.

Ask if anyone can come and write a mathematical sentence for this problem and help the children record:

   1200 + 400 + 600 = ☐

or

   600 + 400 + 1200 = ☐

Problem 2

This time look out for pairs of children who appear to find the answer by:

   adding the 81 and 9 first and then adding 88 and 90.

Discuss this method and why it might be easier than trying to add the 81 and 88 first.

Also discuss how 88 and 90 can be added by using 'compensation' – adding 100 to 88 and then adjusting the answer by subtracting 10.

As before, establish that an appropriate sentence is:

   81 + 88 + 9 = ☐

which is equivalent to:

   81 + 9 + 88 = ☐

This latter arrangement of the numbers means that using an empty number line to support their mental calculation should not be necessary. However, if any children are having difficulty, then model this on the empty number line.

Unit 13

Problem 3

The numbers here are more awkward than those in the previous problems, so encourage the children to use an empty number line to support their reasoning.

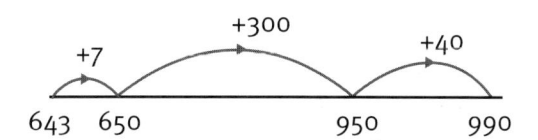

Noting that:

$3 + 7 = 10$

means that adding on the units first is a sensible strategy.

Linking up the problems

Ask the children to look at all three problems and discuss with their partner what they all have in common.

Apart from being about sea creatures, the children should be able to notice that they are all addition problems. Point out to them that two of the problems were change problems where an initial quantity was changed in some way, and one of the problems was a change problem that involved two amounts that needed to be put together or combined to give the final total. Can they identify which was which?

Follow-up problems

Pairs

Give out problem sheets A and B.

As the children are working, encourage them to write down appropriate mathematical sentences.

Question 4 on each sheet is a subtraction problem. The children should not find it difficult to see that this question is different and explain why in Question 6.

Ask any children who finish quickly to write their own combine problem to swap with a partner.

Wrap up

Whole Class

For each sheet, ask the children which one of the questions was not an addition problem and how they knew.

Les bicyclettes

Objectives

- Recognise addition problems as both change and combine
- Use and apply mental strategies for addition

Big Book problems

Like the 'Sea escapades' problems, these three problems have the same structure and are all addition problems. However, the structure of the problems is a little more complicated than in the previous unit. Problem 1 follows the usual structure of an addition problem where the result of combining three quantities has to be found. Problem 3 is an addition as change problem, but rather than finding the result of the change the children have to establish what the change is. Thus, although an addition problem, this could be solved by subtraction. Problem 2 has the most difficult structure. This is another addition as change problem, but the change and end result are given so the children have to find the starting amount.

Whole class

Problem 1

As the children are working, make a note of any pairs who calculate:

$55.5 + 4.5 = \Box$

first and then add the 17. Make sure that one such pair is amongst those invited to come to the front to explain their method.

If no pair has used this method, model it yourself. Use the empty number line to help show the structure of the solution method.

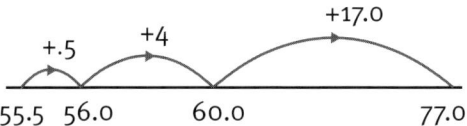

```
        +.5    +4         +17.0
       ⌒     ⌒         ⌒
      55.5  56.0      60.0         77.0
```

Point out the equivalence of the two mathematical sentences:

$17 + 55.5 + 4.5 = \Box$

and

$55.5 + 4.5 + 17 = \Box$

Problem 2

Encourage the children to use an empty number line to support their reasoning here. Two methods of solution are likely:

starting with 122 and adding on to this to reach 275

or

starting at 275 and subtracting 122

If a pair has used either method encourage them to explain their reasoning. Otherwise, model both yourself using an empty number line.

Unit 14

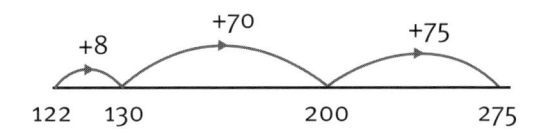

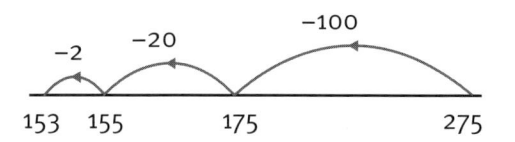

```
        +70                              -100
  +8  ┌──→┐    +75              -20  ┌──────┐
 ┌→┐  │   │  ┌───→┐        -2  ┌──→┐ │      │
 ─┴──┴────┴──┴────┴──      ─┴──┴───┴─┴──────┴──
122 130    200    275      153 155    175      275
```

Discuss with the children that there are three equivalent mathematical sentences linked to the problem:

☐ + 122 = 275

122 + ☐ = 275

275 − 122 = ☐

Problem 3

The structure of this problem makes it likely that the children will count on from 345 to 740. The empty number line is particularly helpful here.

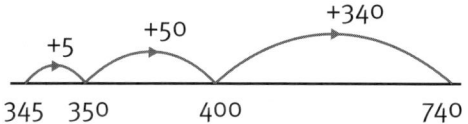

```
                       +50      +340
              +5    ┌───→┐   ┌────────→┐
             ┌→┐    │    │   │         │
             ─┴────┴────┴───┴──────────┴──
            345 350      400            740
```

Discuss the number sentence that arises from this problem:

345 + ☐ = 740

What are other number sentences that are equivalent to this?

Did anyone spot that 345 + 400 = 740 and adjust the answer by taking 5 off 400?

Linking up the problems

Turn back to the page of 'Sea escapades' problems. Ask if anyone can remember what all those problems had in common.

Return to the current problems. Ask the children to look at all three problems and discuss with their partner why they could also all be described as addition problems, even if they used subtraction to solve some of them.

Follow-up problems

Pairs

Give out problem sheets A and B. As the children are working, encourage them to write down appropriate mathematical sentences. Question 5 on each sheet is a multiplication problem. Ask any children who finish quickly to write their own addition problem to swap with a partner.

Wrap up

Whole class

For each sheet, ask the children to explain why they thought Question 5 was different to the rest.

Gnoming around

Objectives
- Recognise compare problems (difference) as subtraction
- Use and apply mental strategies for subtraction

Big Book problems

Whole class

All three problems here can be solved by subtraction. All three are subtraction situations that involve comparing two amounts and finding the difference. In Problems 1 and 2 this is reasonably clear. Problem 3 is more complicated as the difference is given rather than having to be found. Each of the problems can be modeled either by adding on or subtracting.

Problem 1

For this first problem, ask the children NOT to work out the answer, but simply to write down the mathematical sentence that they are going to find the answer to in order to solve the problem. The children should not have too much difficulty in establishing:

$6.5 - 2.2 = \Box$

as an appropriate sentence.

Now ask them to work out the answer. Invite children to share their methods. If anyone suggests that they found the answer by counting up from 2.2 to 6.5, show how they might have recorded this as:

$2.2 + \Box = 6.5$

Other methods to encourage include subtracting 2 from 6 and then subtracting 2 from 5.

Problem 2

Read out the problem and ask the children to work in pairs to find a solution and to be prepared to explain their method. Strategies that the children are likely to use include

- subtracting 23 from 24, then subtracting .4 from .9 and adding the product back on to the answer
- counting up from 23.4 to 24.9

Unit 15

Establish that there are two different mathematical sentences that they could use to record the calculations:

$$24.9 - 23.4 = \square$$
$$23.4 + \square = 24.9$$

Problem 3

Ask the children to work in pairs to find a solution and to be prepared to explain their method.

Once the children have sorted out the relationship of the height it is likely that they will set up the mathematical sentence:

$$2.8 + \square = 4.3$$

Establish that the situation can also be thought of in terms of subtraction and set up the sentence:

$$4.3 - 2.8 = \square$$

Linking up the problems

Point out to the children that each of the problems could be represented by a subtraction sentence. Explain that all three problems involved some sort of comparing: nothing was taken away or changed, but two sets were compared.

Follow-up problems

Pairs

Give out problem sheets A and B.

As the children are working on the problem sheets, encourage them to write down appropriate mathematical sentences. Encourage children who are having difficulty to set up a diagram of the situation or to model it on the empty number line.

Wrap up

Whole class

Invite children to share with the class the problems that they wrote. Does the class agree that these are compare problems?

Work with the class on writing up a description of the difference between a subtraction as take away problem and a subtraction as compare problem.

Airport

Objectives
- Understand subtraction as 'taking away'
- Identify change problems involving subtraction

Big Book problems

These problems have the same structure as change problems involving a decrease and with the result unknown. Each problem contains a quantity that has to be reduced to find a total amount. The structure of the first two problems is quite straightforward and children should have few difficulties solving them and writing an appropriate mathematical sentence. The third problem is more difficult as it is the amount that was subtracted that has to be calculated, rather than the end amount.

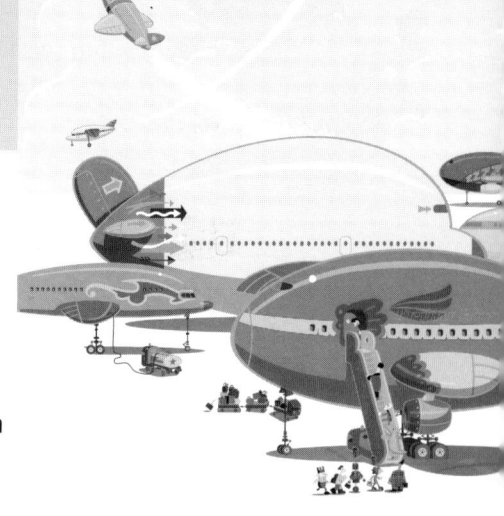

Class

Problem 1

It should be easy for the children in their pairs to relate the 'action' of this problem (that is, part of a quantity being removed) to subtraction and to write down the mathematical sentence

750 − 255 = ☐

As children share their methods, you might want to remind them that an empty number line can help them keep track of their working if they are not confident on holding all the information in their heads. Also support the less confident children to bridge through the 100 in subtracting 35.

If no one spots it, point out to the children that an efficient means of calculating here is to subtract 250 from 750 and then adjust the answer.

Problem 2

Here again, this should not present too many difficulties. Ask one of the children to come and write the mathematical sentence on the board and, if appropriate, show how this could be modelled on the empty number line.

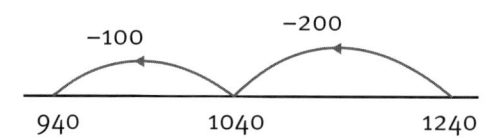

1240 − 300 = ☐

Problem 3

Once pairs have found a solution to this problem, help children use the relationship between addition and subtraction to set up different mathematical sentences:

750 − ☐ = 4000

or

4000 + ☐ = 7500

Unit 16

Discuss with the children which they think is the easier method: counting back from 7500 to 4000 or counting on from 4000 to 7500, or are they equally easy? Point out that although the word problem actually involved taking away, to solve the mathematical sentence they might choose to do something different (count on).

Linking up the problems

Ask the children to look at all three problems and discuss with their partner what they all have in common.

Apart from being about airports, the children should be able to notice that they are all subtraction problems. Point out to them that they are all subtraction as take away problems: that each problem involved an amount that needed to be changed in some way to find the answer.

Follow-up problems

Pairs

Give out problem sheets A and B.

As the children are working, encourage them to write down appropriate mathematical sentences. Encourage children who are having difficulties keeping track of their working to use an empty number line to record their thinking.

Question 3 on each sheet is not really a problem at all. It is there to make the point that they need to read questions carefully and not assume they know what is expected either because of the pattern of the worksheet or because of the numbers involved.

Ask any children who finish quickly to try and write down what is meant by a change problem.

Wrap up

Whole class

Ask children to share with the class the change problems that they wrote. Is everyone convinced that each one is a change problem? How do they know?

Changing Pelts

Objectives
- Recognise multiplication as repeated addition problems
- Use tables to record information

Big Book problems

Whole class

All three problems here are relatively straightforward, being based on multiplication as repeated addition. The children should not have too many difficulties working out what to do to solve the problems. The emphasis in the teaching and discussion should be on the links to recording these as multiplication sentences and effective ways of working out the calculations. Note that throughout this book the convention adopted is that of reading 3 x 4 as 'three multiplied by four' or 'three timesed by four' (that is, three taken four times.)

Problem 1

Ask the children to work either on their own or with a partner to try and figure out the solution to the problem. As they work, make a note of different methods that they use so that you can call upon particular individuals to come and share their method with the class. In particular, watch out for children who need to add together 8 lots of 32 and anyone who carried out the multiplication by 8 by doubling and doubling and doubling again. Work with the children on recording the calculation as:

32 x 8 = 256

Point out that since there were 32 spots in one bag and there were 8 bags that is why you need to add 32 to itself 8 times or multiply 32 by 8.

Did anyone use the fact that 32 x 10 = 320 and subtract 64 from this to find the answer?

Problem 2

Treat this problem in the same way as problem one, establishing the appropriate number sentence of:

42 x 25 = 1050

Children are likely to have found the answer to this in two different ways:

- by multiplying 42 by 10 and then doubling this to get 42 x 20, halving it to get 42 x 5 and adding the two answers
- by multiplying 48 by 100 and then halving the answer and halving again

Discuss both these methods with the children and which they think was easier.

Problem 3

Follow the same approach here as in the previous two problems, setting up the number sentence of:

13 x 15 = 120

Unit 17

Discuss a strategic way of finding the solution to this: 13 × 15 can be found by calculating 13 × 10 and 13 × 5 and adding the two answers together.

Linking up the problems

Go back to Problem 1 and record the working in the form of a simple table:

Bags	Spots
1	32
2	64
4	128
8	256

Record again the associated multiplication 32 × 8. Talk through how, reading down the table, the 1 became 8 times bigger and so the 24 also has been multiplied by 8.

Ask the children to have a go at drawing up the table for the second problem. When they have had a minute or two to do this, work through setting up, using the table to record the intermediate step of multiplying by 100

Boxes	Banana leaves
1	42
100	4200
50	2100
25	1050

Again, talk through the multiplicative relationships between the numbers in the columns: the one becomes 100 times bigger (is multiplied by 100) so the 42 needs to be made 100 times bigger, then the 100 is halved to 50 so the 4200 must be halved and so on. Repeat this for Problem 3.

Boxes	Stripes
1	13
10	130
5	65
15	195

Follow-up problems

Pairs

If children use repeated addition methods to find the answers, get them to record these appropriately (that is, using the addition symbol), and work with them on recording them as multiplications. The children are not expected to put the information into table form, but if you think any of them could cope with this, encourage them to do so.

Wrap up

Whole class

Go over one or two of the problems that the children made up for themselves. Work on recording these as multiplications and also putting the information in the form of a table.

Witsend Towers

Objectives

- Recognise multiplication as rate problems
- Use multiplication rather than repeated addition

Big book problems

Whole class

Although, on the surface, these problems look very similar to multiplication as repeated addition, they are subtly different. While these problems can be solved using repeated addition, the underlying contexts that give rise to the calculations are themselves not repeated addition situations. Here the contexts are all ones where some sort of rate is involved. In the previous unit the total number of items were always present from the beginning: spots in boxes or leaves in cartons. Hence the items could, in theory, be taken out and counted. In rate problems the final number of items does not pre-exist the calculation, but is created within the context.

These differences are not explicitly explored with the children, but the use of relationship tables helps the children develop an intuitive feel for such situations.

Problem 1

Put this partially completed table on the board and ask if anyone can explain the relationship between the table and the information given in the problem:

Number of cars	Number of people
1	7

Discuss how the table shows the number of people that each car can hold. Ask the children how many cars there were in total and how they could build up the table to find the answer.

Number of cars	Number of people
1	7
8	56
16	
32	

Ask the children to discuss with their partner what they think the final missing number in the table should be and why they have come up with that answer. Discuss what the missing number is and establish that it is 224. Leave the table up on the board for the rest of the lesson.

Problem 2

Put this table on the board and ask the children if they can complete the first row:

Number of jaws	Number of people
1	8

Unit 18

Establish that the top row entries should be 1 and 8 as each car can hold 8 people. Ask the children what might be a good intermediate calculation to make in going from 1 car to 14 cars.

Once you have agreed that 7 would be a suitable intermediate step, ask the children to work in pairs to figure out the final number.

Number of jaws	Number of people
1	8
7	
14	

Again, leave the completed table on the board as a prompt for later in the lesson.

Problem 3

Deal with this problem in the same way as Problem 2, putting up the empty table and working with the children on filling in the first row, the first column, multiplying by 9 as an intermediate step and then adding the final missing figure.

Number of boats	Number of people
1	9
9	
18	

Linking up the problems

Direct the children's attention back to Problem 1. Work with the children on recording the calculation that they carried out as: 7 × 32 = 224 (7 people for each one of 32 cars, hence 7 multiplied by 32).

Ask them to work in pairs and to record their calculation for Problem 2 as a multiplication sentence: 8 × 14 = 112 (8 people for every car, 14 cars, hence 8 multiplied by 14). Repeat this for Problem 3, setting up the calculation 9 × 18 = 162. Point out that all three problems are multiplication situations.

Follow-up problems

Pairs

Ask the children to draw up tables for the problems that need them. Warn them that one of the problems does not need a table drawn up, so they will only be drawing up five tables. Problem 4 is the rogue question, not being a problem at all. Some children may feel that they do not need to draw up the tables to find the answer. Acknowledge with them that that is fine, but that they will need to be able to use the tables later so you would like them to draw them up even if they do not feel the need.

Wrap up

Whole class

Ask the children for examples of the problems that they made up using the table in Question 6.

Planting out

Objectives
- Recognise multiplication as array problems
- Use tables to record information

Big Book problems

Whole class

The structure of these three problems is very similar to that of the problems in 'Changing Pelts', but whereas those situations were based on repeated addition, the ones here arise from multiplication as arrays. Once again, simple tables are used to record the information.

Problem 1

Remind the children of the work that you did on the last unit and in particular how the information in the questions could be recorded in the form of a table. Work with the class on setting up an appropriate table for the first problem, with intermediate steps.

Number of rows	Number of potatoes
1	13
20	
5	
25	

Ask the children to work either on their own or with a partner to try and figure out the solution to the problem.

Point out that as there were 13 potatoes in one row and there were 25 rows, that is why you need to multiply 13 by 25. Link this to the table: reading down the table, the 1 became 25 times bigger and so the 13 also has been multiplied by 13.

Problem 2

Treat this problem in the same way as Problem 1, starting off by asking the children to work in pairs and draw up an appropriate table to record the information and intermediate steps.

Number of rows	Number of onion seeds
1	23
10	
30	
4	
34	

As before, establish that the appropriate multiplication sentence is 23 × 34 and link this to reading down the columns of the table: we go from 1 row to 34 rows, so we have multiplied by 34 the 23 tomato plants that there are in one row.

Unit 19

Problem 3

Follow the same approach here as in the previous two problems, setting up the models of:

Number of rows	Number of leek seeds
1	41
100	
50	
2	
52	

41 × 52 (41 multiplied by 52)

Linking up the problems

Go back over the tables drawn up for each problem, recapping on how to interpret these by reading down the columns. Put up the following table:

Number of rows	Number of tomato plants
1	35
29	

Ask the children to talk to their partner for a minute or two and to decide what the wording of the problem might have been that gave rise to this table. Invite children to share their problems with the class.

Follow-up problems

Pairs

The follow-up problems all follow a very similar format to the Big Book problems and the children should not have too many difficulties in finding answers, even if their methods are not the most efficient.

This time the children are expected to put the information into table form. Do not worry if they do this before or after solving the problems, it is simply to get them used to recording the information in this form.

Question 3 is a subtraction problem, there to check that the children are thinking about the wording of the problems and not simply falling into a formulaic approach.

Wrap up

Whole class

Go over one or two of the problems that the children made up for themselves.
Work on recording these as multiplications and checking that they reflect the information in the table.

Planet Zog

Objectives
- Recognise multiplication as scaling problems
- Use and apply knowledge of multiplication bonds

Big Book problems

Whole class

So far, the children have been working on three different models of multiplication: multiplication as repeated addition, multiplication as rate and multiplication as arrays. These three models were linked by putting the information into table form.

This unit deals with the model of multiplication as scaling. Through the context of comparing quantities, children are encouraged to think of such comparisons as a scaling up: in other words, to think of them multiplicatively rather than additively.

Problem 1

Read through this problem with the children and ask them to discuss with a partner what they think the solution is. Invite pairs to explain how they worked out the answer. Did anyone use a table to help them keep track of their workings? In particular, emphasise thinking about the solution as multiplication: Starmike is 16 times as heavy as Mike so Mike's weight of 26 kg needs to be multiplied by 16:

$26 \times 16 = 576$

Problem 2

As with Problem 1, after reading it through with the children get them to discuss the solution in pairs. The important thing to emphasise is the fact that Starmonty is 14 times longer than Monty, so the appropriate mathematical sentence is:

$31 \times 14 = 434$

Problem 3

Treat this problem in the same fashion as Problems 1 and 2. Once again, pay attention to the link between the way in which Starmax is 17 times as heavy as Max and the associated mathematical sentence of:

$18 \times 17 = 126$

Unit 20

Linking up the problems

Ask the children to work in pairs and discuss what is similar about all three problems. Draw out the key idea that each problem involves making a comparison between two quantities. Point out to the children that the problems did not say how much heavier or longer the visitors were, but instead indicated how many times heavier or longer they were. Encourage the children to use the language of scaling: that the weight of Mike needed to be scaled up by a multiple of 16. Can the children use the language of scaling to talk about the other problems in a similar way?

Follow-up problems

Pairs

All but one of the problems follows a similar format in dealing with scalings. However, Question 5 is different in that it is an addition problem rather than a scaling problem.

Wrap up

Whole class

Discuss with the children their solutions.

Verger Records

Objectives
- Recognise division as repeated subtraction (grouping)
- Recognise the relationship between multiplication and division

Big Book problems

This is the first of the Year 6 units dealing with division. This unit works on the model of division as repeated subtraction. This is complemented in the next unit by the model of division as 'sharing': given £45, if this is spent on 6 items each costing the same amount, how much does each item cost?

Whole Class

Problem 1

In pairs, ask the children to work together and figure out the answer. Invite children to offer their solutions and methods of arriving at them. Remind them of the sorts of tables they have been drawing up and ask them to draw up a table to represent the information in the problem.

Number of videos	Total cost
1	£6.25
	£43.75

It is likely that many children will have solved this problem by implicitly saying 'what do I need to multiply 6.25 by to get 43.75?'

$6.25 \times \square = 43.75$

As the relationship between the numbers here is not immediately obvious, the solution can be found by adding in intermediate steps

Number of videos	Total cost	
1	£6.25	
2	£12.50	
4	£25.00	(still £18.75 to get to £43.75)
6	£37.50	(still £6.25 to get to £43.75)
7	£43.75	

Problem 2

Again, set the pairs off to work out the solution. As before, get some children to share their methods. Work with the class on drawing up a relationship table to model the second problem and compare it with the first. Work with the class on establishing that an appropriate table is:

Number of CDs	Total cost
1	£7.50
	£45

Unit 21

and that there are two ways of thinking about the missing number:

> down the columns – what do you have to multiply the £7.50 by to get to £45?
>
> or
>
> across the rows: the one has been scaled up to 7.50 so the 45 must be divided by 7.50

In this case, thinking down the columns is easier and the children may want to fill in some additional steps. Leave the table on the board for the children to refer to.

Number of CDs	Total cost
1	£7.50
2	£15
6	£45

Problem 3

Ask the children to draw up a relationship table and appropriate calculations. Go over their solutions, discussing how they could use the information to find the solution.

Number of DVDs	Total cost
1	£9.99
	£79.92

Encourage children here to work out intermediate steps by rounding the £9.99 to £10 and adjusting the answer.

Number of DVDs	Total cost	
1	£9.99	
5	£49.95	(£10 x 5 – 5p)
3	£29.97	(still £29.97 to get to £79.92)
8	£79.92	(£10 x 3 – 5p)

Linking up the problems

Ask the children to discuss with their partner what is common to the three problems. Discuss with the class that both are division problems and involve building up equal costs. In each case they were told how much had been spent in total and how much each item cost and they had to find out how many items were bought.

Follow-up problems

Pairs

Give out problem sheets A and B. As the children are working, encourage them to write down appropriate mathematical sentences and reinforce the idea that they can use either multiplication or division to reach a solution.

Wrap up

Whole class

Invite two or three pairs to share their problems with the class. Can the class decide when they think it is more appropriate to use division rather than multiplication?

Party time

Objectives
- Recognise division as sharing problems
- Use and apply the relationship between multiplication and division

Big Book problems

Whole class

This is the second of the units dealing with division. In contrast to the previous unit, this works on the model of division as sharing. This is likely to be a more familiar model for the children and Problems 1 and 2 should not present them with too many difficulties.

Problem 3 is like the ones in the previous units and is a division as repeated subtraction (grouping). Careful use of relationship tables should help the children to sort out the information in the problems. Some of these problems are also two-step problems.

Problem 1

In pairs, ask the children to work together and figure out the answer. The first thing they have to do is work out the total number of sandwiches. Invite children to offer their solutions and methods of arriving at them. Once again, remind them of the sorts of tables they have been drawing up and ask them to draw up a table to represent the information in the problem. Work with the class on establishing that an appropriate table is:

Number of plates	Number of sandwiches
1	
20	180

It is likely that many children will have solved this problem by saying 'what do I need to multiply 20 by to get 180?' and working with trial and improvement.

$20 \times \square = 180$

This relates to the figures in the table by reading 'across' the table, noting that whatever the 20 had to be multiplied by to get 180, the 1 in the first column has to be multiplied by the same number to preserve the relationship.

Point out that the table can also be read up from bottom to top: the relationship of the 20 to the 1 is that the 1 is 20 times smaller, or the 20 is divided by 20. So the 180 must also be divided by 20:

$180 \div 20 = \square$

This number sentence can be solved by subtracting multiples of 20 from 180.

Leave the table on the board for the children to refer to.

Problem 2

Again, set the pairs off to work out the solution. Here they do have to start by adding the numbers of sweets together. As before, get some children to share their methods. Work

Unit 22

with the class on drawing up a relationship table to model the second problem and comparing it with the first

Number of bags	Number of sweets
1	
30	360

As in Problem 1, explore the relationships between reading down the columns of the table and across the rows.

Problem 3

Ask the children to draw up a relationship table and appropriate calculations for this problem. This time, they do not have to add together the number off muffins and doughnuts.

The structure of this problem is different from the previous one. As children complete their tables, encourage them to talk about them in different ways: across the rows from left to right and right to left, up and down the columns.

Number of tables	Number of muffins
1	12
	156

One way to tackle the solution here is put in additional rows and multiply up to 84.

Number of tables	Number of muffins
1	12
10	120
3	36
	156

(36 away from the total of 156)

Follow-up problems

Pairs

Give out problem sheets A and B. Three of the problems are division as sharing problems while the other two are division as equal grouping or repeated subtraction problems. In both cases, drawing up relationship tables should help the children keep track of the information.

As the children are working, encourage them to write down appropriate mathematical sentences and reinforce the idea that they can use either multiplication or division to reach a solution depending on how they 'read' the information in their tables.

Wrap up

Whole class

Discuss the two different models of multiplication: repeated subtraction (equal grouping) and sharing. Can the children explain how they would be able to tell the difference between the two?

Dan the Dragon Slayer

Objectives

- Understanding division as repeated subtraction
- Deciding whether to round up or round down an answer, depending on the context

Big book problems

Whole class

These problems introduce the children to the need to look at the mathematical solution to a problem and decide whether or not that is a sensible solution to the contextual situation from which the calculation arose. This is done using division problems where there is a need to either round up or round down the numerical answer to arrive at a sensible solution.

Problem 1

Set the pairs off to work out the solution. As they are working, note the different methods they use and select the two or three pairs that you will invite to demonstrate their method.

When two or three methods have been shown, ask the children what number sentence(s) they could write to express the calculation they carried out. Put these on the board. Some may suggest 20 × 12 = 240 and if it is not forthcoming from the children, put up 248 ÷ 10 = 12 r 8.

Discuss with the children the difference between the mathematical solution (12 r 8) and the problem solution and whether the sensible answer to the problem is 12 r 8, 12 or 13.

Problem 2

Repeat the above for Problem 3. Once again, get 250 ÷ 12 = 20 r 10 on the board and discuss what the sensible answer to the problem is (21).

Problem 3

As before, set the pairs off to work out the solution. As they are working, note the different methods they use and select the two or three pairs that you will invite to demonstrate their method.

Once again, some may suggest 15 × 13 = 345 and if it is not forthcoming from the children, put up 350 ÷ 15 = 13 r 5.

Discuss with the children the difference between the mathematical solution (13 r 5) and the problem solution and whether the sensible answer to the problem is 13 r 5, 13 or 14.

Unit 23

Linking up the problems

Ask the children in their pairs to discuss and jot down:

- ways in which the problems are alike
- ways in which problems are different

Discuss their various suggestions for similarities and differences. In particular, draw out:

- all the problems involved division
- the answers to 1 and 2 were rounded up, while the answer to 3 was rounded down

Follow-up problems

Pairs

Give out problem sheets A and B.

The children work out the solutions, and decide whether they had to round up or round down to give a sensible answer to the problem.

As the children are working, encourage them to write down appropriate mathematical sentences and reinforce the idea that repeated subtraction leads to division.

Question 4 on each sheet is a subtraction problem, so that the children do not assume that all the questions are division ones.

Wrap up

Whole class

Invite two or three pairs to share their problems with the class. Can the class decide which is the 'round up' problem and which is the 'round down' problem?

Display other pairs of problems on the problem board, with the invitation to decide which are round up problems and which are round down.

Lords of the Bling

Objectives
- Recognise which operation to use when solving word problems
- Consolidate different problem classifications

This unit presents a 'mixed bag' of problems. As the children work on them, they need to be encouraged to see if they can remember if the problems are like any that they have encountered before.

Big Book problems

Whole Class

As the children work through each problem in turn, concentrate on discussing the calculation strategies that they used. Then, when they have finished all three problems, discuss what type of problem each was.

Problem 1

This is a two stage problem. The first is a multiplication as rate problem and the children should not have too much difficulty in setting up the calculation:

14 × 11

It will help reinforce the link between this and multiplication problems if you set up a table to show the information.

Number of gold rings	Number of good luck charms
1	14
11	

The second stage of the problem is to find out how many of the 200 rings are left over. Watch out for children who think that they have got the answer when they've found the answer to 14 × 11.

Problem 2

This is a division as sharing problem. Again, it will help reinforce the link between this and multiplication problems if you set up a table to show the information.

Number of gold chains	Number of potions
1	
6	84

Children can find the missing number either by solving:

84 ÷ 6 = ☐

or

☐ × 6 = 84

Unit 24

Problem 3

This is a three step problem. First two multiplication as rate problems need to be calculated:

$6 \times 15 = \square$

and

$5 \times 18 = \square$

The two products then need to be added.

The final, easy to overlook step is to add in 2 for Brodo and Bagno!

Linking up the problems

Ask the children to work in pairs and discuss what type of problem each one was. Can they remember any of the names for different types of problems introduced over the previous lessons?

Problems 1 and 2 are both rate problems, one involving multiplication and the other division. Problem 3 involves rates as well, but has several steps to keep track of.

Follow-up problems

Pairs

As well as finding solutions to the problems, the children should try and identify what type of problem each example represents. The best way to structure this would be to get them to work on their own to solve the problems and then to work in pairs and discuss each one in turn to decide what type of problem it is.

Questions 1, 3 and 4 are all rate problems; Question 2 is change (subtraction); Question 5 is also a subtraction, but is finding the difference; Question 6 is a simple multiplication, but with several distracting pieces of information.

Wrap up

Whole Class

Go over the follow-up problems, discussing what type each one is.

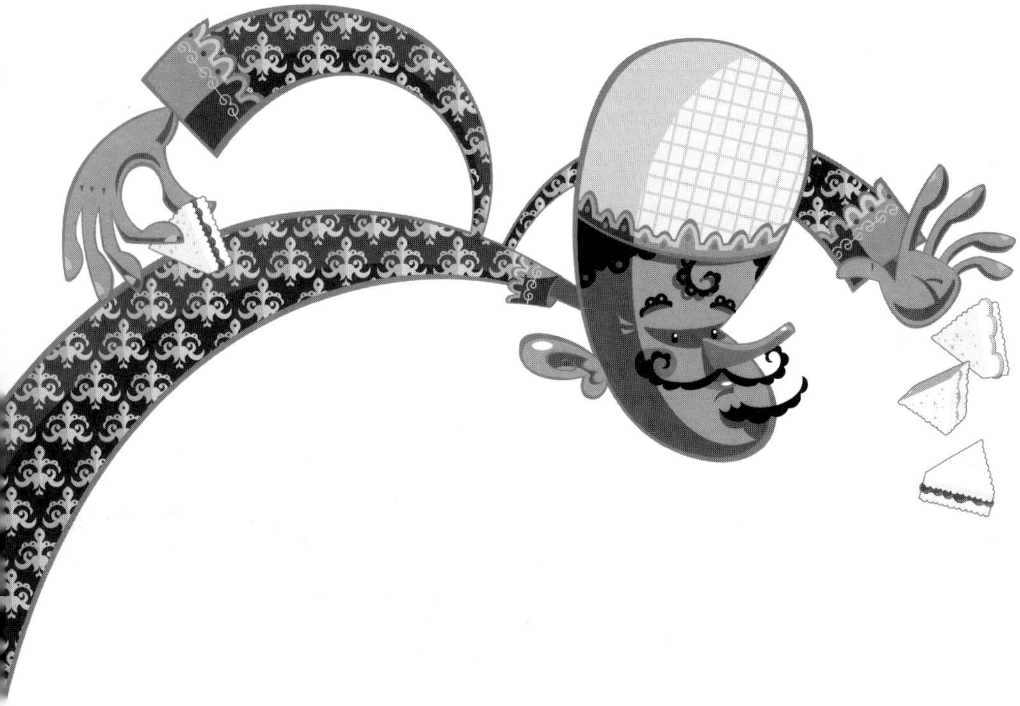

Unit problem sheets

Year 5

- Unit 1 **Snowball**
- Unit 2 **Family shopping**
- Unit 3 **Snakes and Adders**
- Unit 4 **Cyclops**
- Unit 5 **Clown capers**
- Unit 6 **The magic cupboard**
- Unit 7 **Percy the builder**
- Unit 8 **Gardener's World**
- Unit 9 **Village fête**
- Unit 10 **Gods and goddesses**
- Unit 11 **Reunion**
- Unit 12 **Thor, the god of thunder**

Year 6

- Unit 13 **Sea escapades**
- Unit 14 **Les bicyclettes**
- Unit 15 **Gnoming around**
- Unit 16 **Airport**
- Unit 17 **Changing Pelts**
- Unit 18 **Witsend Towers**
- Unit 19 **Planting out**
- Unit 20 **Planet Zog**
- Unit 21 **Verger Records**
- Unit 22 **Party time**
- Unit 23 **Dan the Dragon Slayer**
- Unit 24 **Lords of the Bling**

Snowball

Unit 1/A

1. The seagulls flew in for the annual snowball.
   258 wore yellow socks and 364 wore orange socks.
   How many seagulls were wearing socks?

2. 52 penguins were sliding on the ice. 354 joined in
   the sliding, then another 8 bold penguins started sliding.
   How many penguins were sliding?

3. 294 seals each ate a cod fish finger and 59 ate
   a haddock fish finger. How many fish fingers got eaten?

4. 186 polar bears got into a snowball fight.
   129 got hit by snowballs. How many polar bears
   escaped getting hit by snowballs?

5. 189 seals were sunbathing on an ice floe.
   Another 31 seals jumped on to join them,
   but the ice floe sank and all the seals fell into the water.
   How many seals ended up in the water?

6. One of the problems above was not an addition problem.
   Which one was it? What sort of problem was it
   and how do you know?

BEAM's Big Book of Word Problems © BEAM Education

Snowball

Unit 1/B

1. The seagulls flew in for the annual snowball.
   253 wore yellow socks and 344 wore orange socks.
   How many seagulls were wearing socks?

2. 52 penguins were sliding on the ice. 144 joined in
   the sliding, then another 8 bold penguins started sliding.
   How many penguins were sliding?

3. 224 seals each ate a cod fish finger and 59 ate
   a haddock fish finger. How many fish fingers got eaten?

4. 186 polar bears got into a snowball fight.
   29 got hit by snowballs. How many polar bears
   escaped getting hit by snowballs?

5. 69 seals were sunbathing on an ice floe.
   Another 31 seals jumped on to join them,
   but the ice floe sank and all the seals fell into the water.
   How many seals ended up in the water?

6. One of the problems above was not an addition problem.
   Which one was it? What sort of problem was it
   and how do you know?

BEAM's Big Book of Word Problems © BEAM Education

Family shopping

Unit 2/A

1. Victoria bought a hat, size 6, for £17.65 and a pair of shoes, size 30, for £28.35. How much did she spend?

2. David was going out to buy a coat. He had some money in his pocket and he put in another £6.25. On the way to the shop, all the money fell out through a hole in his pocket. When David counted the money that fell out there was £14. How much money was in his pocket before David put in the £6.25?

3. Romeo wanted to buy a book. He had £12.19. The book cost £21. How much more money did Romeo need?

4. Brooklyn went out shopping with £31. When he got home, he had £9.15 left. How much did he spend?

5. Cruz bought 11 T-shirts and a pair of shorts. Each T-shirt cost £2.99 and the shorts cost £13.99. How much did Cruz spend on T-shirts?

6. One of the problems above involved using a different mathematical operation to the others. Which problem was it? Was the operation addition, subtraction, multiplication or division?

BEAM's Big Book of Word Problems © BEAM Education

Family shopping

Unit 2/B

1. Victoria bought a hat, size 6, for £15.65 and a pair of shoes, size 30, for £24.35. How much did she spend?

2. David was going out to buy a coat. He had some money in his pocket and he put in another £6.50.
On the way to the shop, all the money fell out through a hole in his pocket. When David counted the money that fell out there was £13.
How much money was in his pocket before David put in the £6.50?

3. Romeo wanted to buy a book. He had £12.50. The book cost £20. How much more money did Romeo need?

4. Brooklyn went out shopping with £30. When he got home, he had £9.50 left. How much did he spend?

5. Cruz bought 10 T-shirts and a pair of shorts. Each T-shirt cost £2.99 and the shorts cost £13.99. How much did Cruz spend on T-shirts?

6. One of the problems above involved using a different mathematical operation to the others.
Which problem was it? Was the operation addition, subtraction, multiplication or division?

Snakes and Adders

Unit 3/A

1. Gertie Fields is 270 cm long. She hopes to grow to be as long as her sister, Gracie. Gracie is 460 cm long. How many centimetres more does Gertie need to grow?

2. Annie Adder is 629 cm long and weighs 360 g. Annie's mum, Adele, is 712 cm long and weighs 540 g. How much does Annie need to grow to be as long as her mum?

3. Robbie Rattler is 52 cm longer than his brother Rupert and 650 g heavier. Robbie weighs 940 g. How heavy is Rupert?

4. Penny Python weighs 5250 g and is 1750 cm long. Penny's son, Pat, is 18 months old and 860 cm long. How much longer is Penny than Pat?

5. Coral Cobra can rise up to a height of 76 cm, but her friend Camille can only rise up to 59 cm. How much higher can Coral raise herself?

6. Use this information to make up a compare problem:

   Sam Snake is 450 cm long and weighs 380 g.

   Sid Snake is 640 cm long and weighs 530 g

BEAM's Big Book of Word Problems © BEAM Education

Snakes and Adders

Unit 3/B

1. Gertie Fields is 250 cm long. She hopes to grow to be as long as her sister, Gracie. Gracie is 480 cm long. How many centimetres more does Gertie need to grow?

2. Annie Adder is 630 cm long and weighs 360 g. Annie's mum, Adele, is 750 cm long and weighs 540 g. How much does Annie need to grow to be as long as her mum?

3. Robbie Rattler is 52 cm longer than his brother Rupert and 650 g heavier. Robbie weighs 950 g. How heavy is Rupert?

4. Penny Python weighs 5250 g and is 1680 cm long. Penny's son, Pat, is 18 months old and 840 cm long. How much longer is Penny than Pat?

5. Coral Cobra can rise up to a height of 75 cm, but her friend Camille can only rise up to 60 cm. How much higher can Coral raise herself?

6. Use this information to make up a compare problem:

   Sam Snake is 430 cm long and weighs 320 g

   Sid Snake is 650 cm long and weighs 560 g

Cyclops

Unit 4/A

1. Cyclops was walking along a forest path that was 14800 m long. There were 245 garlic plants growing along the path edge and Cyclops pulled up 75 and ate them. How many garlic plants were left growing?

2. Cyclops spotted a galleon at anchor offshore. There were 220 sailors on board the galleon. Cyclops counted 45 men getting in a boat and coming to shore. How many sailors were left on board the galleon?

3. 78 sailors left on board the galleon fell asleep after drinking too much rum.
   39 of the other sailors jumped overboard for a swim. How many sailors fell asleep?

4. Cyclops chopped down 345 trees. He used 69 of the chopped-down trees to build a fence and used the rest to make a huge bonfire. How many trees were on the bonfire?

5. Cyclops caught 235 wild horses, but then decided to let 76 go free. How many wild horses was he left with?

6. What was special about Question 3? Can you use the information in Question 3 to make up a change problem?

BEAM's Big Book of Word Problems

© BEAM Education

Cyclops

Unit 4/B

1. Cyclops was walking along a forest path that was 14800 m long. There were 265 garlic plants growing along the path edge and Cyclops pulled up 55 and ate them. How many garlic plants were left growing?

2. Cyclops spotted a galleon at anchor offshore. There were 250 sailors on board the galleon. Cyclops counted 45 men getting in a boat and coming to shore. How many sailors were left on board the galleon?

3. 78 sailors left on board the galleon fell asleep after drinking too much rum.
39 of the other sailors jumped overboard for a swim.
How many sailors fell asleep?

4. Cyclops chopped down 380 trees. He used 49 of the chopped-down trees to build a fence and used the rest to make a huge bonfire. How many trees were on the bonfire?

5. Cyclops caught 265 wild horses, but then decided to let 85 go free. How many wild horses was he left with?

6. What was special about Question 3? Can you use the information in Question 3 to make up a change problem?

Clown capers

Unit 5/A

1. Coco ordered 8 boxes of flashing bow ties. Each bow tie had 25 spots on it. Each box contained 16 bow ties. Coco unpacked the bow ties and tried them all on to check that they worked. How many bow ties did Coco try on?

2. An order of 45 boxes of stink bombs arrived. There were 36 stink bombs in each box. Coco threw each stink bomb on the floor to see if it worked. How many stink bombs did Coco throw on the floor?

3. Red noses come packed in boxes of 28. Coco was carrying 20 boxes of red noses when she sneezed and dropped 14 boxes. All the red noses in the 14 boxes fell out. How many red noses bounced across the floor?

4. Red-hot sweets are packed 9 to a bag and Coco had 21 bags on her shelf. One day, while she was working, Coco ate 15 bags of red-hot sweets. How many red-hot sweets did she eat?

5. Coco had an order for 300 packets of itching powder. She had 16 boxes of itching powder and each box contained 12 packets of itching powder. How many more packets of itching powder does Coco need for her order?

6. Make up your own problem about Coco.

Clown capers

Unit 5/B

1. Coco ordered 10 boxes of flashing bow ties. Each bow tie had 25 spots on it. Each box contained 15 bow ties. Coco unpacked the bow ties and tried them all on to check that they worked. How many bow ties did Coco try on?

2. An order of 30 boxes of stink bombs arrived. There were 24 stink bombs in each box. Coco threw each stink bomb on the floor to see if it worked. How many stink bombs did Coco throw on the floor?

3. Red noses come packed in boxes of 25. Coco was carrying 20 boxes of red noses when she sneezed and dropped 12 boxes. All the red noses in the 12 boxes fell out. How many red noses bounced across the floor?

4. Red-hot sweets are packed 6 to a bag and Coco had 21 bags on her shelf. One day, while she was working, Coco ate 12 bags of red-hot sweets. How many red-hot sweets did she eat?

5. Coco had an order for 200 packets of itching powder. She had 15 boxes of itching powder and each box contained 10 packets of itching powder. How many more packets of itching powder does Coco need for her order?

6. Make up your own problem about Coco.

The magic cupboard

Unit 6/A

1. Every time Marge left a kiwi fruit in her cupboard for a month, the kiwi fruit turned into 8 worms. One month, Marge left 14 kiwi fruit in her cupboard. How many worms did she find?

2. When Marge left a lemon in her cupboard it turned into 7 maggots. If Marge put away 18 lemons, how many maggots would they turn into?

3. Putting a peach into the magic cupboard turned it into 9 flies. Marge picked 21 peaches off the tree in her garden and put them in her cupboard. How many flies did she find a month later?

4. Putting a strawberry in the cupboard for a month turned it into 6 maggots. Marge forgot that she had put 23 strawberries in the cupboard. How many maggots did she find a month later?

5. If Marge puts a nectarine in her magic cupboard, it turns into 17 flies. One morning, Marge put 33 nectarines in her cupboard. She took 17 out again later that day to make a fruit salad. How many nectarines were left in the cupboard?

6. Use the information in this table to make up a problem.

Number of blueberries	Number of flies
1	11
13	

The magic cupboard

Unit 6/B

1. Every time Marge left a kiwi fruit in her cupboard for a month, the kiwi fruit turned into 6 worms. One month, Marge left 12 kiwi fruit in her cupboard. How many worms did she find?

2. When Marge left a lemon in her cupboard it turned into 5 maggots. If Marge put away 16 lemons, how many maggots would they turn into?

3. Putting a peach into the magic cupboard turned it into 9 flies. Marge picked 11 peaches off the tree in her garden and put them in her cupboard. How many flies did she find a month later?

4. Putting a strawberry in the cupboard for a month turned it into 6 maggots. Marge forgot that she had put 15 strawberries in the cupboard. How many maggots did she find a month later?

5. If Marge puts a nectarine in her magic cupboard, it turns into 17 flies. One morning, Marge put 36 nectarines in her cupboard. She took 15 out again later that day to make a fruit salad. How many nectarines were left in the cupboard?

6. Use the information in this table to make up a problem.

Number of blueberries	Number of flies
1	11
13	

BEAM's Big Book of Word Problems

© BEAM Education

Percy the builder

Unit 7/A

1. Percy was tiling a bathroom floor. The floor was 13 tiles long and 17 tiles wide. Percy bought ten boxes of tiles. Each box of tiles contained 20 tiles. How many tiles did Percy have left over?

2. Percy put tiles up on a kitchen wall. The wall was 28 tiles long and 14 tiles high. How many tiles did Percy need?

3. Percy decided to build a wall across his garden, and then a brick barbecue. He had 200 bricks delivered. Percy built the wall 13 bricks long and 9 bricks high. How many bricks did Percy have left to build his barbecue with?

4. Percy ordered 175 white tiles and 180 black tiles for a bathroom floor. The floor was 17 tiles wide and 18 tiles long. How many tiles did Percy order altogether?

5. Percy put paving stones down in his garden. The garden is 23 paving stones wide and 17 paving stones long. Each paving stone weighs 4500 g and costs £1.35. How many paving stones did Percy need?

6. Make up your own problem about Percy.

BEAM's Big Book of Word Problems © BEAM Education

Percy the builder

Unit 7/B

1. Percy was tiling a bathroom floor. The floor was 12 tiles long and 15 tiles wide. Percy bought ten boxes of tiles. Each box of tiles contained 20 tiles. How many tiles did Percy have left over?

2. Percy put tiles up on a kitchen wall. The wall was 25 tiles long and 12 tiles high. How many tiles did Percy need?

3. Percy decided to build a wall across his garden, and then a brick barbecue. He had 200 bricks delivered. Percy built the wall 12 bricks long and 11 bricks high. How many bricks did Percy have left to build his barbecue with?

4. Percy ordered 145 white tiles and 150 black tiles for a bathroom floor. The floor was 17 tiles wide and 18 tiles long. How many tiles did Percy order altogether?

5. Percy put paving stones down in his garden. The garden is 20 paving stones wide and 15 paving stones long. Each paving stone weighs 4500 g and costs £1.35. How many paving stones did Percy need?

6. Make up your own problem about Percy.

BEAM's Big Book of Word Problems © BEAM Education

Gardener's World

Unit 8/A

1. On Monday, Sid's pumpkin weighed 72 g. A week later it was 7 times as heavy. How heavy was Sid's pumpkin then?

2. Jolene's sunflower was 28 cm tall when she first measured it. 8 days later, it was 6 times as tall. How tall was the sunflower then?

3. When Nigel first weighed his favourite courgette, it weighed only 9 g. But when he next weighed it, it was 21 times as heavy. Was Nigel correct when he said he had a courgette that weighed more than half a kilogram?

4. Elizabeth counted that there were 58 strawberries on her strawberry plant. 10 days later, there were 6 times as many strawberries on the plant. How many strawberries was that?

5. Joe was growing a marrow. When he first weighed it, the marrow weighed 78 g. Three days later, it weighed 18 g more. How much did it then weigh?

6. Joe said that the answer to Question 5 is found by calculating 78 × 18. Explain why Joe is wrong.

BEAM's Big Book of Word Problems

© BEAM Education

Gardener's World

Unit 8/B

1. On Monday, Sid's pumpkin weighed 42 g. A week later it was 5 times as heavy. How heavy was Sid's pumpkin then?

2. Jolene's sunflower was 30 cm tall when she first measured it. 8 days later, it was 5 times as tall. How tall was the sunflower then?

3. When Nigel first weighed his favourite courgette, it weighed only 10 g. But when he next weighed it, it was 21 times as heavy. Was Nigel correct when he said he had a courgette that weighed more than half a kilogram?

4. Elizabeth counted that there were 54 strawberries on her strawberry plant. 10 days later, there were 5 times as many strawberries on the plant. How many strawberries was that?

5. Joe was growing a marrow. When he first weighed it, the marrow weighed 75 g. Three days later, it weighed 12 g more. How much did it then weigh?

6. Joe said that the answer to Question 5 is found by calculating 75 × 12. Explain why Joe is wrong.

Village fête

Unit 9/A

1. Nigella was pouring out cups of tea. She unpacked 20 cups. She had 360 ml of tea. Nigella poured 40 ml of tea into each cup. How many cups did Nigella fill?

2. Gordon was putting fudge into bags. He put 25 g of fudge into each bag. Gordon started out with 275 g of fudge. How many bags did he fill?

3. Jamie was cutting up sticks of rock into small pieces. Each stick of rock was 42 cm long. If each small piece that he cut off was 6 cm long, and he had 7 sticks of rock, how many small pieces did he end up with?

4. Ainsley was putting toffees into bags. For each bag he weighed out 35 g of toffee. If he filled 17 bags, how much did all the toffee weigh?

5. Make up a problem using the information in the table below. Find the answer to your problem.

Number of bags	Amount of sherbert
1	12 g
	144 g

6. Make up a problem using the information in the table below. Find the answer to your problem.

Number of bags	Number of cakes
1	6
	96

BEAM's Big Book of Word Problems © BEAM Education

Village fête

Unit 9/B

1. Nigella was pouring out cups of tea. She unpacked 20 cups. She had 350 ml of tea. Nigella poured 50 ml of tea into each cup. How many cups did Nigella fill?

2. Gordon was putting fudge into bags. He put 20 g of fudge into each bag. Gordon started out with 240 g of fudge. How many bags did he fill?

3. Jamie was cutting up sticks of rock into small pieces. Each stick of rock was 30 cm long. If each small piece that he cut off was 5 cm long, and he had 6 sticks of rock, how many small pieces did he end up with?

4. Ainsley was putting toffees into bags. For each bag he weighed out 30 g of toffee. If he filled 15 bags, how much did all the toffee weigh?

5. Make up a problem using the information in the table below. Find the answer to your problem.

Number of bags	Amount of sherbert
1	12 g
	24 g

6. Make up a problem using the information in the table below. Find the answer to your problem.

Number of bags	Number of cakes
1	6
	66

BEAM's Big Book of Word Problems © BEAM Education

Gods and goddesses

Unit 10/A

1. Melone, the goddess of happiness, has 14 arms.
   She holds the same number of stars in each hand.
   Melone can pick up 210 stars altogether.
   How many stars does Melone hold in each hand?

2. Fiori, the god of nature, holds 12 flowers in each of his hands.
   Altogether, Fiori holds 264 flowers. How many hands
   does Fiori have?

3. Cresta, the snow god, has 18 arms, 24 legs and 3 heads.
   She holds the same number of icicles in each hand.
   Altogether, Cresta holds 432 icicles. How many icicles
   does she hold in each hand?

4. Cremolo, the god of seeing, has many heads.
   Each head has 9 candles on it. Altogether, Cremolo has
   189 candles on his heads. How many heads does
   Cremolo have?

5. Suspicia is the god of secrets. She has 16 hands
   and each hand holds the same number of boxes.
   Altogether, Suspicia holds 240 boxes. How many boxes
   does Suspicia hold in each hand?

6. Sort the above problems into two groups:

   division as sharing problems

   division as grouping (repeated subtraction) problems

BEAM's Big Book of Word Problems © BEAM Education

Gods and goddesses

Unit 10/B

1. Melone, the goddess of happiness, has 8 arms.
   She holds the same number of stars in each hand.
   Melone can pick up 160 stars altogether.
   How many stars does Melone hold in each hand?

2. Fiori, the god of nature, holds 12 flowers in each of his hands.
   Altogether, Fiori holds 180 flowers. How many hands
   does Fiori have?

3. Cresta, the snowgod, has 8 arms, 24 legs and 3 heads.
   She holds the same number of icicles in each hand.
   Altogether, Cresta holds 240 icicles. How many icicles
   does she hold in each hand?

4. Cremolo, the god of seeing, has many heads.
   Each head has 6 candles on it. Altogether, Cremolo has
   90 candles on his heads. How many heads does
   Cremolo have?

5. Suspicia is the god of secrets. She has 16 hands
   and each hand holds the same number of boxes.
   Altogether, Suspicia holds 80 boxes. How many boxes
   does Suspicia hold in each hand?

6. Sort the above problems into two groups:

   division as sharing problems

   division as grouping (repeated subtraction) problems

BEAM's Big Book of Word Problems

© BEAM Education

Reunion

Unit 11/A

1. 46 old school friends went to the seaside. 4 people could travel in each car. What was the smallest number of cars the friends needed to travel in to make sure that everyone got to the seaside?

2. The 46 friends decided to organise a sandcastle-building competition. Each sandcastle-building team had to have 4 builders. How many complete teams were they able to form?

3. They bought a carton of 60 cans of cola to drink. Each of the 46 friends drank 1 can of cola. How many cans were left over?

4. The 46 friends also bought some packets of cookies. Each packet contained 6 cookies. How many packets did they need to open so that everyone got a cookie?

5. 8 of the friends went off to collect shells. They collected 75 shells. They put exactly 9 shells into each bag. How many bags did they fill?

6. Make up two division problems:

    one where you need to round down the answer to the problem

    one where you need to round up the answer to the problem

Reunion

Unit 11/B

1. 30 old school friends went to the seaside. 4 people could travel in each car. What was the smallest number of cars that the friends needed to travel in to make sure that everyone got to the seaside?

2. The 30 friends decided to organise a sandcastle-building competition. Each sandcastle building team had to have 4 builders. How many complete teams were they able to form?

3. They bought a carton of 48 cans of cola to drink. Each of the 30 friends drank 1 can of cola. How many cans were left over?

4. The 30 friends also bought some packets of cookies. Each packet contained 8 cookies. How many packets did they need to open so that everyone got a cookie?

5. 8 of the friends went off to collect shells. They collected 75 shells. They put exactly 10 shells into each bag. How many bags did they fill?

6. Make up two division problems:

   one where you need to round down the answer to the problem

   one where you need to round up the answer to the problem

BEAM's Big Book of Word Problems © BEAM Education

Thor, the god of thunder   *Unit 12/A*

1. A thundercloud released 249 ml of water each minute. If the storm lasted for 6 minutes, how many litres of water did the cloud release?

2. 210 bolts of lightning were in the clouds. 119 bolts of lightning were released in the storm. How many bolts of lightning were still in the clouds?

3. The wind was blowing at 7 km per hour. Thor swung his hammer and the wind became 14 times faster. How fast was the wind blowing then?

4. There was a lightning flash every 15 seconds. If the storm lasted for a minute and a half, how many lightning flashes were there?

5. Thor rode through the skies on his horse for an hour and travelled 189 km. He was travelling to Valhalla, which was 350 km away. How much further did Thor have to travel?

6. At the Valhalla feast, Thor drank 30 flasks of ale and ate 24 steaks. Each steak weighed 300 grams and each flask of ale contained 200 ml of ale. How much would 12 steaks weigh?

Thor, the god of thunder — Unit 12/B

1. A thundercloud released 250 ml of water each minute. If the storm lasted for 5 minutes how many litres of water did the cloud release?

2. 240 bolts of lightning were in the clouds. 119 bolts of lightning were released in the storm. How many bolts of lightning were still in the clouds?

3. The wind was blowing at 5 km per hour. Thor swung his hammer and the wind became 15 times faster. How fast was the wind blowing then?

4. There was a lightning flash every 15 seconds. If the storm lasted for a minute, how many lightning flashes were there?

5. Thor rode through the skies on his horse for an hour and travelled 189 km. He was travelling to Valhalla, which was 400 km away. How much further did Thor have to travel?

6. At the Valhalla feast, Thor drank 30 flasks of ale and ate 24 steaks. Each steak weighed 300 grams and each flask of ale contained 200 ml of ale. How much would 10 steaks weigh?

Sea escapades

Unit 13/A

1. 72 crabs set out for a walk. On the way, they met another 56 crabs who joined in the walk. Then 28 more joined in. How many crabs were out on the walk?

2. 1500 clown fish were swimming. They met up with a shoal of another 350 clown fish. Finally, 650 more clown fish joined in the swim. How many clown fish ended up swimming together?

3. 548 great turtles swam alongside a pod of 249 dolphins. How many turtles and dolphins were swimming together?

4. 432 barracudas were swimming when they came across a sunken ship. 269 of the barracudas swam inside the ship. How many did not swim inside the ship?

5. 379 sea snails crawled into a cave. Inside, they found another 149 sea snails. How many sea snails were inside the cave?

6. One of the problems above was not an addition problem. Which one was it. What sort of problem was it and how do you know?

Sea escapades

Unit 13/B

1. 70 crabs set out for a walk. On the way, they met another 55 crabs who joined in the walk. Then 30 more joined in. How many crabs were out on the walk?

2. 1500 clown fish were swimming. They met up with a shoal of another 300 clown fish. Finally, 700 more clown fish joined in the swim. How many clown fish ended up swimming together?

3. 750 great turtles swam alongside a pod of 249 dolphins. How many turtles and dolphins were swimming together?

4. 400 barracudas were swimming when they came across a sunken ship. 349 of the barracudas swam inside the ship. How many did not swim inside the ship?

5. 399 sea snails crawled into a cave. Inside they found another 199 sea snails. How many sea snails were inside the cave?

6. One of the problems above was not an addition problem. Which one was it. What sort of problem was it and how do you know?

BEAM's Big Book of Word Problems
© BEAM Education

Les bicyclettes

Unit 14/A

1. Jules and Jim set out on holiday from Toulouse. On day one, they cycled 29 km and then stopped for 225 ml each of lemonade. They then cycled 38.5 km before stopping for another 175 ml each of lemonade. They cycled a final 15 km before stopping, when they each had a final 280 ml of lemonade. How much lemonade did they each drink?

2. On day two, they cycled all morning and by lunch they had cycled 89 km. They hoped to have cycled 175 km altogether by the end of the day. How far did they need to cycle in the afternoon?

3. By the end of day three, Jules and Jim had cycled a total of 328 km. They noted that by the end of day four they had cycled a total of 417 km. How far did they cycle on day four?

4. On day five, they turned around to return home. Their shorter route home was 365 km and they cycled 91 km. How far from home were they at the end of day five?

5. Before setting off on day six, Jules did his morning exercises. He did 8 sets of 15 press-ups, ran on the spot for 10 minutes, skipped for 15 minutes and then did another 4 sets of 15 press-ups. How many press-ups did Jules do altogether?

6. One of the problems above involved using a different mathematical operation to the others. Which problem was it? Was the operation addition, subtraction, multiplication or division?

BEAM's Big Book of Word Problems © BEAM Education

Les bicyclettes

Unit 14/B

1. Jules and Jim set out on holiday from Toulouse. On day one, they cycled 29 km and then stopped for 200 ml each of lemonade. They then cycled 38.5 km before stopping for another 150 ml each of lemonade. They cycled a final 15 km before stopping, when they each had a final 250 ml of lemonade. How much lemonade did they each drink?

2. On day two, they cycled all morning and by lunch they had cycled 79 km. They hoped to have cycled 182 km altogether by the end of the day. How far did they need to cycle in the afternoon?

3. By the end of day three, Jules and Jim had cycled a total of 331 km. They noted that by the end of day four they had cycled a total of 450 km. How far did they cycle on day four?

4. On day five, they turned around to return home. Their shorter route home was 400 km and they cycled 89 km. How far from home were they at the end of day five?

5. Before setting off on day six, Jules did his morning exercises. He did 8 sets of 15 press-ups, ran on the spot for 10 minutes and skipped for 15 minutes. How many press-ups did Jules do altogether?

6. One of the problems above involved using a different mathematical operation to the others. Which problem was it? Was the operation addition, subtraction, multiplication or division?

Gnoming around

Unit 15/A

1. Groucho threw a stick weighing 55 g a distance of 13.4 m. Zeppo found a stick weighing 78 g and threw it 9.7 m. How much further did Groucho throw his stick?

2. Chico jumped 26.9 m carrying a stone that weighed 7.9 kg. Harpo picked up a stone that weighed 11.3 kg and jumped 31.2 m. How much heavier was the stone that Harpo picked up than the one that Chico picked up?

3. Chico is 3.7 kg lighter than Zeppo. Chico weighs 19.6 kg. How much does Zeppo weigh?

4. Groucho is 4.6 kg heavier than Harpo. Groucho weighs 22.3 kg. How heavy is Harpo?

5. Groucho is 29 cm shorter than Zeppo and Zeppo is 17 cm shorter than Chico. Groucho is 34 cm tall. How tall is Chico?

6. Make up a problem using some of this information:

   Groucho is 78 years old
   Chico is 93 years old

   Zeppo weighs 35.6 kg
   Chico weighs 43.8 kg

BEAM's Big Book of Word Problems

© BEAM Education

Gnoming around

Unit 15/B

1. Groucho threw a stick weighing 55 g a distance of 13.7 m.
   Zeppo found a stick weighing 78 g and threw it 9.4 m.
   How much further did Groucho throw his stick?

2. Chico jumped 26.5 m carrying a stone that weighed 8.3 kg.
   Harpo picked up a stone that weighed 11.6 kg
   and jumped 31.7 m. How much heavier was the stone
   that Harpo picked up than the one that Chico picked up?

3. Chico is 3.4 kg lighter than Zeppo. Chico weighs 16.2 kg.
   How much does Zeppo weigh?

4. Groucho is 4.3 kg heavier than Harpo. Groucho weighs
   26.6 kg. How heavy is Harpo?

5. Groucho is 9 cm shorter than Zeppo and Zeppo is 17 cm
   shorter than Chico. Chico is 34 cm tall. How tall is Groucho?

6. Make up a problem using some of this information:

   Groucho is 78 years old
   Chico is 93 years old

   Zeppo weighs 35.6 kg
   Chico weighs 43.8 kg

BEAM's Big Book of Word Problems © BEAM Education

Airport

Unit 16/A

1. 782 passengers arrived on a jumbo jet at Hat-trick airport at 19:30.
   596 passengers got off, but the rest had to wait in the plane as they were flying on to Lupin airport.
   How many passengers were left on the plane?

2. At 14:15, 639 passengers were waiting by departure gates 83 to 86 at Hat-trick airport.
   356 of these passengers were told to go to gate 94.
   How many passengers were left at gates 83 to 86?

3. At 12:30, there were 265 passengers at gate 45.
   15 minutes later, another 27 passengers arrived.
   10 minutes later, they were told that their flight was delayed, so 58 passengers went to get a drink.
   How many passengers were at gate 45 at 12:30?

4. 738 passengers were in a queue at passport control. Another checking desk opened and 246 passengers were directed to queue there. How many passengers were left in the first queue?

5. 6332 passengers were in the airport at 12:00. By 13:00, there were 4655 passengers remaining in the airport. How many passengers had taken off between 12:00 and 13:00?

6. Make up your own airport problem involving subtraction.

BEAM's Big Book of Word Problems

© BEAM Education

Airport

Unit 16/B

1. 796 passengers arrived on a jumbo jet at Hat-trick airport at 19:30.
   582 passengers got off, but the rest had to wait in the plane as they were flying on to Lupin airport.
   How many passengers were left on the plane?

2. At 14:15, 656 passengers were waiting by departure gates 83 to 86 at Hat-trick airport.
   329 of these passengers were told to go to gate 94.
   How many passengers were left at gates 83 to 86?

3. At 12:30, there were 265 passengers at gate 45.
   15 minutes later, another 27 passengers arrived.
   10 minutes later, they were told that their flight was delayed, so 58 passengers went to get a drink.
   How many passengers were at gate 45 at 12:30?

4. 746 passengers were in a queue at passport control. Another checking desk opened and 232 passengers were directed to queue there. How many passengers were left in the first queue?

5. 6889 passengers were in the airport at 12.00. By 13.00, there were 4655 passengers remaining in the airport. How many passengers had taken off between 12:00 and 13:00?

6. Make up your own airport problem involving subtraction.

BEAM's Big Book of Word Problems © BEAM Education

Changing Pelts

Unit 17/A

1. Tony wanted new stripes. A box of stripes contains 17 stripes. Tony put 20 boxes in his trolley, but then put 3 boxes back on the shelf. How many stripes did Tony buy?

2. Charlie wanted some tea bags. Tea bags come in packets of 36. Charlie bought 9 packets of tea bags and 0.5 l of milk. How many tea bags did Charlie buy?

3. Sheal was buying shells for a new floor. She bought 48 boxes of shells. Each box weighed 150 g and contained around 60 shells. How much did the 48 boxes weigh all together?

4. Rhonnie needed some bags of mud. One small bag of mud weighs 1500 g and a large sack of mud weighs 15 kg. Rhonnie bought 8 sacks of mud and 5 small bags. What weight of mud did Rhonnie buy?

5. Bombi wanted a new hay bed. Each bale of hay weighed 17 kg. Bombi bought 13 bales of hay and took them home. That was not enough hay so she went back for 7 more bales. What was the total weight of hay that Bombi bought?

6. Use the information in this table to make up a problem.

Number of bags	Number of coconuts in a bag
1	17
18	

BEAM's Big Book of Word Problems

© BEAM Education

Changing Pelts

Unit 17/B

1. Tony wanted new stripes. A box of stripes contains 15 stripes. Tony put 20 boxes in his trolley, but then put 5 boxes back on the shelf. How many stripes did Tony buy?

2. Charlie wanted some tea bags. Tea bags come in packets of 36. Charlie bought 11 packets of tea bags and 0.5 l of milk. How many tea bags did Charlie buy?

3. Sheal was buying shells for a new floor. She bought 50 boxes of shells. Each box weighed 150 g and contained around 60 shells. How much did the 50 boxes weigh all together?

4. Rhonnie needed some bags of mud. One small bag of mud weighs 1500 g and a large sack of mud weighs 15 kg. Rhonnie bought 10 sacks of mud and 2 small bags. What weight of mud did Rhonnie buy?

5. Bombi wanted a new hay bed. Each bale of hay weighed 15 kg. Bombi bought 7 bales of hay and took them home. That was not enough hay so she went back for 3 more bales. What was the total weight of hay that Bombi bought?

6. Use the information in this table to make up a problem.

Number of bags	Number of coconuts in a bag
1	17
18	

BEAM's Big Book of Word Problems

© BEAM Education

Witsend Towers

Unit 18/A

1. Each carriage on the Neck-cracker holds 14 people. There are 30 cars, but 2 of them are always kept empty. How many people can ride on the Neck-cracker when it is full?

2. The Knee-knocker can hold 16 people. Each day, the Knee-knocker makes 36 journeys. Each journey covers a distance of 750 m. If it is full on each journey, how many people can ride on the Knee-knocker each day?

3. The Blood-chiller has 27 rows of seats for people to ride in. Each row has 18 seats. You have to be over 120 cm tall to ride the Blood-chiller. How many people can ride on the Blood-chiller when it is full?

4. The Plunge-down drops from a height of 200 m. 16 people can ride each time. It takes 90 seconds for the carriage to rise to the top and 6 seconds for it to plunge down.
How far does the Plunge-down drop?

5. The Flying Saucer has 9 spokes and there are 4 carriages on the end of each spoke. 6 people can ride in each carriage. How many people can ride on the Flying Saucer when it is full?

6. Use the information in this table to make up and answer a problem.

Number of carriages	People in a carriage
1	12
24	

BEAM's Big Book of Word Problems

© BEAM Education

Witsend Towers

Unit 18/B

1. Each carriage on the Neck-cracker holds 15 people.
   There are 32 cars but 2 of them are always kept empty.
   How many people can ride on the Neck-cracker when it is full?

2. The Knee-knocker can hold 16 people. Each day,
   the Knee-knocker makes 25 journeys. Each journey covers
   a distance of 750 m. If it is full on each journey, how many
   people can ride on the Knee-knocker each day?

3. The Blood-chiller has 27 rows of seats for people to ride in.
   Each row has 18 seats. You have to be over 120 cm tall
   to ride the Blood-chiller. How many people can ride on
   the Blood-chiller when it is full?

4. The Plunge-down drops from a height of 200 m. 16 people can
   ride each time. It takes 90 seconds for the carriage to rise to
   the top and 6 seconds for it to plunge down.
   How far does the Plunge-down drop?

5. The Flying Saucer has 9 spokes and there are 4 carriages
   on the end of each spoke. 6 people can ride in each carriage.
   How many people can ride on the Flying saucer
   when it is full?

6. Use the information in this table to make up and answer
   a problem.

Number of carriages	People in a carriage
1	12
15	

BEAM's Big Book of Word Problems

© BEAM Education

Planting out

Unit 19/A

1. Gladys had 4 bags of 250 turnip seeds. She planted out 38 rows with 22 seeds in each row. How many turnip seeds did she have left over?

2. Gladys was planting out carrots. She put 16 carrots in each row. Gladys planted out 37 rows from a bag of 600 carrots. How many carrots did she plant out?

3. Gladys started off the day with a bag of 750 seed potatoes. By the end of the day, she had planted out 490 seed potatoes in rows of 14. How many seed potatoes did she have left?

4. Gladys had a bag of 3000 lettuce seeds. She planted a row of 53 seeds and calculated that there was enough room for 62 rows. Did Gladys have enough seeds?

5. Courgette seeds come in small packets of 28 and large packets of 84. Gladys ordered 18 small packets and 22 large packets. How many seeds was that altogether?

6. Make up your own problem about Gladys.

Planting out

Unit 19/B

1. Gladys had 4 bags of 250 turnip seeds. She planted out 40 rows with 25 seeds in each row. How many turnip seeds did she have left over?

2. Gladys was planting out carrots. She put 15 carrots in each row. Giles planted out 35 rows from a bag of 600 carrots. How many carrots did she plant out?

3. Gladys started off the day with a bag of 750 seed potatoes. By the end of the day she had planted out 440 seed potatoes in rows of 14. How many seed potatoes did she have left?

4. Gladys had a bag of 3000 lettuce seeds. She planted a row of 50 seeds and calculated that there was enough room for 55 rows. Did Gladys have enough seeds?

5. Courgette seeds come in small packets of 30 and large packets of 90. Gladys ordered 15 small packets and 20 large packets. How many seeds was that altogether?

6. Make up your own problem about Gladys.

Planet Zog

Unit 20/A

1. Jen woke to find some visitors in her room. Starjen looked a bit like Jen, but was 38 times as old as Jen. Jen is 17 years old. How old is Starjen?

2. Moggy weighs 895 g. Starmoggy is 28 times as heavy as Moggy. How heavy is Starmoggy?

3. Starmax has 123 times as many teeth as Max. Max has 34 teeth. How many teeth has Starmax?

4. Starjen is 14 times as tall as Jen. Jen is 156 cm tall. How tall is Starjen?

5. Starspring was 46 cm tall when crouching down. When Starspring stood up, she was 77 cm taller. How tall was Starspring when she was standing up?

6. Jo said that the answer to Question 5 is found by calculating 46 × 77. Explain why Jo is wrong.

BEAM's Big Book of Word Problems

© BEAM Education

Planet Zog

Unit 20/B

1. Jen woke to find some visitors in her room. Starjen looked a bit like Jen, but was 35 times as old as Jen. Jen is 15 years old. How old is Starjen?

2. Moggy weighs 999 g. Starmoggy is 30 times as heavy as Moggy. How heavy is Starmoggy?

3. Starmax has 120 times as many teeth as Max. Max has 30 teeth. How many teeth has Starmax?

4. Starjen is 15 times as tall as Jen. Jen is 160 cm tall. How tall is Starjen?

5. Starspring was 46 cm tall when crouching down. When Starspring stood up, she was 77 cm taller. How tall was Starspring when she was standing up?

6. Jo said that the answer to Question 5 is found by calculating 46 × 77. Explain why Jo is wrong.

Verger Records

Unit 21/A

1. Memrit found some CDs he had been looking for at £6.49 each. Altogether, he spent £51.92. How many CDs did Memrit buy?

2. Amir bought some music books. Each book cost £11.99 and Amir got 6p change from £72. How many books did Amir buy?

3. Hamsa spent £37.45 on some T-shirts. Each T-shirt cost £7.49. How many T-shirts did Hamsa buy?

4. Jelly went out to buy some DVDs in the sale. She had £48 to spend. Each DVD cost £5.99. How many DVDs could Jelly buy if she spent all her money on these?

5. Make up a problem using the information in the table below. Find the answer to your problem.

Number of CDs	Price
1	£9.99
	£99.90

6. Make up a problem using the information in the table below. Find the answer to your problem.

Number of Books	Price
1	£10.50
	£126

BEAM's Big Book of Word Problems

Verger Records

Unit 21/B

1. Memrit found some CDs he had been looking for at £6.50 each. Altogether, he spent £52. How many CDs did Memrit buy?

2. Amir bought some music books. Each book cost £12 and Amir spent £72. How many books did Amir buy?

3. Hamsa spent £37.50 on some T-shirts. Each T-shirt cost £7.50. How many T-shirts did Hamsa buy?

4. Jelly went out to buy some DVDs in the sale. She had £48 to spend. Each DVD cost £6. How many DVDs could Jelly buy if she spent all her money on these?

5. Make up a problem using the information in the table below. Find the answer to your problem.

Number of CDs	Price
1	£9
	£99

6. Make up a problem using the information in the table below. Find the answer to your problem.

Number of Books	Price
1	£10
	£120

Party time

Unit 22/A

1. Patrick is putting out cakes for the school disco. He has made 146 chocolate cakes and 154 orange cakes. He puts out all the cakes, putting the same number of cakes on each plate. Patrick fills 25 plates. How many sandwiches are on each plate?

2. Anna is setting out the packets of crisps. She has a carton of 154 packets. She puts 14 packets of crisps on on each table. How many tables have crisps on them?

3. Bernice is putting out cans of drink. She has 210 cans of cola and 210 cans of lemonade. There are 35 tables and Bernice puts the same number of cans on each table. How many cans are there on each table?

4. Each table is decorated with same number of balloons. Mark blows up 245 balloons. There are 35 tables. How many balloons can Mark put on each table?

5. Kath puts 18 plates on each serving table. Altogether, she puts out 126 plates. How many serving tables are there?

6. Make up two division problems:

    one with division as sharing

    one with division as equal grouping (repeated subtraction)

BEAM's Big Book of Word Problems © BEAM Education

Party time

Unit 22/B

1. Patrick is putting out cakes for the school disco. He has made 150 chocolate cakes and 50 orange cakes. He puts out all the cakes, putting the same number of cakes on each plate. Patrick fills 25 plates. How many sandwiches are on each plate?

2. Anna is setting out the packets of crisps. She has a carton of 140 packets. She puts 14 packets of crisps on each table. How many tables have crisps on them?

3. Bernice is putting out cans of drink. She has 150 cans of cola and 150 cans of lemonade. There are 30 tables and Bernice puts the same number of cans on each table. How many cans are there on each table?

4. Each table is decorated with same number of balloons. Mark blows up 180 balloons. There are 30 tables. How many balloons can Mark put on each table?

5. Kath puts 20 plates on each serving table. Altogether, she puts out 140 plates. How many serving tables are there?

6. Make up two division problems:

   one with division as sharing

   one with division as equal grouping (repeated subtraction)

BEAM's Big Book of Word Problems © BEAM Education

Dan the Dragon Slayer

Unit 23/A

1. Dan the Dragon Slayer put his collection of bats' wings into an album. Each page in his album could display 14 bats' wings. Over the years, Dan had collected 200 bats' wings. How many pages of his album could he fill?

2. Dan had collected 345 unicorns' horns.
   He put the horns into boxes, putting 20 horns into each box. How many boxes did Dan need?

3. Dan stored larks tongues in bottles. He had 380 larks' tongues and each bottle held 15 larks' tongues. How many bottles did Dan need to store all of his larks' tongues?

4. Dan was checking over his collection of 238 fireflies. The fireflies come in 12 different colours. While he was checking them, 49 of the fireflies flew away. How many fireflies was Dan left with?

5. Dan was using his toads' warts to make jars of skin cream. Each jar of skin cream needed 17 toads' warts. Dan had 200 toads' warts. How many jars of skin cream could he make?

6. Make up two division problems:

   one where you need to round down the answer to the problem

   one where you need to round up the answer to the problem

BEAM's Big Book of Word Problems © BEAM Education

Dan the Dragon Slayer

Unit 23/B

1. Dan the Dragon Slayer put his collection of bats' wings into an album. Each page in his album could display 15 bats' wings. Over the years, Dan had collected 160 bats' wings. How many pages of his album could he fill?

2. Dan had collected 350 unicorns' horns. He put the horns into boxes, putting 20 horns into each box. How many boxes did Dan need?

3. Dan stored larks' tongues in bottles. He had 310 lark's tongues and each bottle can hold 15 larks' tongues. How many bottles did Dan need to store all of his larks' tongues?

4. Dan was checking over his collection of 250 fireflies. The fireflies come in 12 different colours. While he was checking them, 49 of the fireflies flew away. How many fireflies was Dan left with?

5. Dan was using his toads' warts to make jars of skin cream. Each jar of skin cream needed 12 toads' warts. Dan had 130 toads' warts. How many jars of skin cream could he make?

6. Make up two division problems:

    one where you need to round down the answer to the problem

    one where you need to round up the answer to the problem

Lords of the Bling

Unit 24/A

1. Bagno gave Pesta 9 gold bangles. In return, Pesta gave Bagno 333 flying pills. How many flying pills was each gold bangle worth?

2. Brodo was wearing all of his precious gold chains. They were so heavy that he gave some to Bagno to wear. The chains he gave to Bagno weighed 2450 g. Brodo was left wearing chains that weighed 3 kg 780 g. What weight of gold was Brodo wearing before he gave some to Bagno?

3. Pesta offered 28 good luck charms for every one of Brodo's gold toe rings. Brodo handed over his 34 toe rings to Pesta. How many good luck charms did Pesta have to give him?

4. Pesta gave Bagno 306 sleeping potions for gold earrings. The deal was 17 sleeping potions for each earring. How many earrings did Bagno give to Pesta?

5. Bagno was counting his pills and potions. He had 459 flying pills and 388 sleeping potions. He needed 720 flying pills to change for one Sword of Might. How many more flying pills does Bagno need to get before he can get a Sword of Might?

6. Pesta invited some friends round for tea. She put out 12 plates of sugar mice and 15 plates of chocolate frogs. A sugar mouse weighs 28 g and a chocolate frog weighs 32 g. Each plate had 25 things on it. Sugar mice come in boxes of 12 and chocolate frogs in bags of 5. All the sugar mice that Pesta put out got eaten, but only half the chocolate frogs got eaten. How many sugar mice did Pesta put out on plates?

BEAM's Big Book of Word Problems

© BEAM Education

Lords of the Bling

Unit 24/B

1. Bagno gave Pesta 9 gold bangles. In return, Pesta gave Bagno 270 flying pills. How many flying pills was each gold bangle worth?

2. Brodo was wearing all of his precious gold chains. They were so heavy that he gave some to Bagno to wear. The chains he gave to Bagno weighed 2500 g. Brodo was left wearing chains that weighed 3450 g. What weight of gold was Brodo wearing before he gave some to Bagno?

3. Pesta offered 16 good luck charms for every one of Brodo's gold toe rings. Brodo handed over his 30 toe rings to Pesta. How many good luck charms did Pesta have to give him?

4. Pesta gave Bagno 300 sleeping potions for gold earrings. The deal was 15 sleeping potions for each earring. How many earrings did Bagno give to Pesta?

5. Bagno was counting his pills and potions. He had 459 flying pills and 388 sleeping potions. He needed 760 flying pills to change for one Sword of Might. How many more flying pills does Bagno need to get before he can get a Sword of Might?

6. Pesta invited some friends round for tea. She put out 12 plates of sugar mice and 15 plates of chocolate frogs. A sugar mouse weighs 28 g and a chocolate frog weighs 32 g. Each plate had 20 things on it. Sugar mice come in boxes of 12 and chocolate frogs in bags of 5. All the sugar mice that Pesta put out got eaten, but only half the chocolate frogs got eaten. How many sugar mice did Pesta put out on plates?

BEAM's Big Book of Word Problems

© BEAM Education

With thanks to the BEAM Development Group